"David Dockery is the doyen of Christian higher education, having served as a mentor and role model for countless educators over the course of the past several decades. Dr. Dockery is a strong convictional leader and scholar whose strength is undergirded by wisdom and grace. *Convictional Civility* bears witness to this strength, wisdom, and grace, and for that reason, I highly recommend it."

—*Bruce Riley Ashford,* provost and dean of faculty; associate professor of theology and culture, Southeastern Baptist Theological Seminary

"The title of this volume perfectly reflects the commitments of the honoree: David Dockery is a man of robust theological convictions, but no less committed to discourse characterized by civility. One inevitably recalls Paul's exhortation to truth and love. The essays in this volume are diverse in character and scope; several assess Dockery's contributions. But it is the theme of the book as a whole that is compelling, for it stands athwart twin monsters of our age—anemic theological sentimentality on the one hand, and bad-tempered ignorant dogmatism on the other—and cries 'Stop!' by showing a better way."

—*D. A. Carson,* research professor of New Testament, Trinity Evangelical Divinity School

"Reading this *festschrift* that honors the contributions of David Dockery to Christian higher education and to broader kingdom work, I was reminded of a book by Tom Rath titled *Vital Friends: The People You Can't Afford to Live Without.* Friends and colleagues can certainly call out the best in one another, and this impressive collection of essays by friends of the Dockerys conveys the ripple effects of these faithful servant-leaders who have influenced so many lives for the better. At a time when Christian higher education and, indeed, our world need convictional civility as never before, this volume has much to offer. Heartfelt thanks, David and Lanese Dockery, for your faithfulness in showing the way!"

—*Karen A. Longman,* professor and program director, Doctoral Higher Education, Azusa Pacific University

"David Dockery's careful biblical thinking, generous spirit, academic vision, wise leadership, and personal warmth shine through these snapshots of his life, theology, and service. A must read if you, like I, have been significantly impacted by this evangelical and Baptist statesman."

—*Christopher W. Morgan,* dean and professor of
Theology, California Baptist University

"For many of us in the business of Christian higher education, David Dockery has been a model in the way he has combined firm evangelical convictions, broad-based ecumenical charity, and unusual academic insight. Now, as he heads northwards after very productive years at Union University, this book reveals why I am delighted as a 'Yankee evangelical' that he has come over to help us. "

—*Mark Noll,* Francis A. McAnany Professor of History,
University of Notre Dame

"David Dockery is an extraordinary Christian leader and gentleman. These essays are a fitting tribute because they both honor him for his own convictional civility and encourage the same faithful Christian engagement in others. I am grateful to recommend this volume."

—*Thom S. Rainer,* president and CEO, LifeWay Christian Resources

"David Dockery is one of America's most outstanding college presidents. His transformational leadership has been characterized by the rare combination of virtues that this volume celebrates and promotes: Christian charity, theological orthodoxy, and moral integrity."

—*Philip Ryken,* president, Wheaton College

Edited by C. Ben Mitchell, Carla D. Sanderson, and Gregory A. Thornbury

CONVICTIONAL CIVILITY

ENGAGING THE CULTURE IN THE 21st CENTURY

Essays in honor of

DAVID S. DOCKERY

B&H
ACADEMIC
NASHVILLE, TENNESSEE

Convictional Civility:
Engaging the Culture in the 21st Century
Essays in Honor of David S. Dockery

Copyright © 2015 by C. Ben Mitchell, Carla D. Sanderson, and
Gregory Alan Thornbury

B&H Publishing Group

Nashville, Tennessee

ISBN: 978–1–4336–8508–8

Dewey Decimal Classification: 248:5

Subject Heading: CHRISTIAN LIFE \ WITNESSING

Printed in the United States of America

1 2 3 4 5 6 7 8 9 10 • 20 19 18 17 16 15

SB

Contents

Foreword . . . . *vii*
Carla D. Sanderson

ESSAYS

David Samuel Dockery:
Evangelical Baptist and the Doctrine of the Bible *3*
James Leo Garrett Jr.

With David Dockery Among Baptists and Evangelicals *11*
Timothy George

Toward Convictional Civility *19*
Millard J. Erickson

Convictional Clarity *35*
R. Albert Mohler Jr.

What God Hath Joined Together *47*
Robert Smith Jr.

Leadership Lessons from David S. Dockery *67*
Gene C. Fant Jr.

Higher Education's Role in Developing a Civil Society *81*
Hunter Baker

Imaging God Through Union with Christ *95*
Autumn Alcott Ridenour

Baptists, Conscience, and Convictional Civility in Health Care *109*
C. Ben Mitchell

Afterword *123*
Gregory Alan Thornbury

TRIBUTES

A Word of Gratitude and Thanksgiving for David and Lanese Dockery . *133*
    Daniel L. Akin

Conviction, Courage, and Civility. *137*
    Barry H. Corey

Winsome Champion for the Long Sweep of the Christian Intellectual
Tradition. *141*
    Philip W. Eaton

Irenic Conservative, Orthodox Baptist. *145*
    Nathan A. Finn

A Civil "Wedge" in the World. *149*
    George H. Guthrie

Wholehearted Conviction and Winsome Civility *153*
    Barbara C. McMillin

Cultural Warrior, Intellectual Strategist, and Recognized Visionary *157*
    Carol Swain

Activist for Racial Reconciliation *161*
    Kimberly Thornbury

Friend, Mentor, and Guide *165*
    Jon R. Wallace

Faithful Servant *169*
    James Emery White

Generous, Wise, and Humble *171*
    John D. Woodbridge

Learning from a Master. *173*
    Carl Zylstra

David S. Dockery: Professional Highlights (1984–2014). *177*

Contributors. *187*

Name Index *189*

Subject Index *192*

Scripture Index *193*

Foreword

Carla D. Sanderson

On the occasion of his transition from the presidency of Union University—a presidency marked by profound transformation in every indicator characteristic of excellence and quality—a handful of admirers have come together in this *festschrift* to honor David Samuel Dockery, the consummate academic and eminent scholar. A *festschrift* is a celebratory publication. But the Latin phrase for such a work is also fitting: *liber amicorum*, "a book of friends." For at the heart of the matter, the friendship we share with David Dockery has inspired this book.

Let us note: this volume is not intended to signify the pinnacle of Dockery's career, his retirement, or his culminating work as a senior statesman. It is not the placement of a period on his legacy but rather the placement of a commemorative semicolon.

Our team of contributors made up of colleagues, former students, and members of David Dockery's leadership team have enjoyed a festival of writing reflective of his vision for contemporary engagement where witness is more important than winning and fidelity is more effective than fighting.

David Dockery was the first person I heard use the phrase "convictional civility." Everything the man says follows from his work as a Bible scholar, and such is the case with this phrase. Convictional civility is a lifestyle of bearing witness for Christ and of contributing to the common good. From the pulpit to the public square and from the campus to the courtroom, followers of Christ are to demonstrate Christian virtues through winsome civility and Christian values through wholehearted conviction.

This volume is divided into two parts. The first part includes essays featuring original research and informed perspective from respected and seasoned Christian leaders as well as former students who explore convictional civility through their disciplinary or vocational lenses. The second part features congratulatory tributes noting Dockery's influence on the lives and leadership of those endeared to him, extending to him best wishes and gratitude.

James Leo Garrett Jr. begins with a review of Dockery's life and works, giving focus to his contributions in biblical hermeneutics and the doctrine of Scripture. In a beautiful treatise on friendship, Timothy George explains how the two were inspired to pursue a shared dream, taking up their responsibility for theological revival through a shared vision for unity among Baptists and for Baptist solidarity with the larger evangelical world. Millard J. Erickson offers a practical guide that models Dockery's precision of thought and expression. He provides steps to follow—such as self-understanding, empathy, and genuine listening—toward embracing convictional civility as a model for engaging our culture. R. Albert Mohler Jr. reminds us that God has commissioned his church to be faithful truth-tellers, speaking with convictional clarity in a secularized culture that rejects the moral authority of the God of the Bible. Robert Smith Jr. presents a sermon using Paul's ministry of proclamation and witness, exegesis and experience, as an example of the "toughness, tenderness, and tears" required in our day. Gene C. Fant Jr. demonstrates how the Union University community found a leader worth following in Dockery and learned to follow conviction born from the calling that is our own. Testimony is given to how orthodoxy yields both hopefulness and optimism, even in the hard times like the tornado crisis that hit Union during Dockery's tenure. Hunter Baker offers commentary on our Christian civilization, demonstrating how religion and education are the sustenance of our nation. He makes a case for the role Christian higher education plays in developing the civic muscle necessary to liberty. Autumn Alcott Ridenour challenges us to think about moral action, based on an Augustinian and Barthian interpretation, imaging God through union with Christ and union with fellow believers. Finally, C. Ben Mitchell delves into Baptist history, likening our forefathers' advocacy for religious liberty to the expression of conviction that a civil society must accommodate. He draws out the implications for convictional civility to the growing threats to rights of conscience faced by today's health-care providers.

In the celebratory tributes to Dockery, readers will find inspiration in the descriptions of his qualities and characteristics: patient listening and perceptive filtering; graciousness of spirit; promoting solidarity for Christian values and principles in the secular world; prioritizing family and friendship; standing by others in times of crisis; the ability to encourage, uplift, and leave one in awe; the leadership to show how the Christian worldview can influence and galvanize Christ followers. The tributes also describe the challenging contexts of Dockery's formative years and leadership: racial tension in the South during his youth; the resurgence of biblical conservatism in his early years as a scholar; his launch of a Christian higher education movement in the midst of secularization, globalization, and pluralization during his first tenure as a college president; and his quest for renewal and revitalization for Southern Baptists specifically and for the larger church more generally. In the classroom, from the pulpit, through the written word, and out of the boardroom has come visionary and transformative leadership.

I cannot identify the single, most important way in which David Dockery has influenced my life and work. I treasure the memories of the banter before leadership team meetings on topics ranging from sports and politics to denominational polity and evangelical news. Meetings started with a focus on birthdays, anniversaries, illnesses, and deaths of great leaders and Christian thinkers, many alive today and some long dead, but also on every person known as a member of the Union University community. I cherish the praying, hymn singing, movie discussions, book studies, ping-pong matches, meals, and laughter. I am thankful for his endurance with my shortcomings and his forbearance with us as a community. I am thankful for his patience in never overestimating what we could accomplish in one year, and I am thankful for his steadfastness in never underestimating what we could accomplish in five years.

I marvel at Dockery the intellectual, his insight and vision, his unwavering commitment and constant eye on the goal. I am grasped by his mind and his example in seeing everything in life—everything—through the lens of a learned faith and a deep theological understanding of human history. I cherish *Renewing Minds: Serving Church and Society Through Christian Higher Education* (B&H Academic, 2007), the playbook for Union University and a guide for life.

I marvel at the hands and heart of Lanese Huckeba Dockery. Learning from her example of biblical womanhood is my life goal. She is relational like Miriam; inspirational, accessible, wise, and collaborative like Deborah; loyal, hardworking, and determined like Ruth; patient, prayerful, and devoted like Hannah; facilitative, collaborative, and courageous like Esther; industrious, assertive, and hospitable like Martha; long-suffering and steadfast like Mary Magdalene; a good steward of influence like Lydia; and one who prioritizes a love relationship with Jesus like Mary of Bethany.

I am better because of Dockery's leadership, especially the fully orbed view of incremental change that led to transformation: the framing, filtering, defining, and communicating required in change; the stewardship of vision and influence; the dependence on God; the inspiration from and reliance on Scripture; the reasoning together; the risk taking; the informed decision making; the establishing of a plan; and the dogged determination to carry it out. I am better because of the challenge placed on my role as provost. Dockery often said of us, "The Union University faculty is the best teaching faculty in the nation." He said it, and we worked hard to live up to his expectations. His leadership over faculty development has most profoundly transformed Union over two decades of time. The most enduring application of convictional civility to me is Dockery's deep belief in what higher education must be if we are to claim Christ as its head, combined with his gentle, tender, and compelling approach in making it happen. The leadership he modeled is *sine qua non* for the future of Christian higher education and Christian engagement in the world.

To use a few Wendell Berry phrases, I am "captured by gratitude" to have been appointed Union University provost by David Dockery. He has a profound "standing in my eyes" as a Baptist, evangelical, and Christian higher education statesman. I have experienced "God's plenty" for having been close to his leadership, and I feel the ending of our time of service together "like an amputation."

Thank you, DSD. You have forever transformed my alma mater and enhanced her reputation and reach into the broader evangelical world. It is a beautiful place, inside and out. Thank you for the work you have done for my denomination: you have solidified and enhanced the work of the church through theologically informed commitments made to Southern Baptists and to Tennessee Baptists in particular. Most of all, thank you for generations of Union University graduates who are convictional and committed believers, standing in strong pulpits and seated in pews, zealous for the faith of the gospel of Jesus Christ. Our world is a better place because of them.

When I am old, I will say that the 1995–2014 years were the best years of my professional life, thanks to David S. Dockery. "I think it not in my brain only, but in my heart and in all the lengths of my bones."[1]

---

[1] Wendell Berry, *Jayber Crow* (Washington, DC: Counterpoint, 2000), 310.

Essays

David Samuel Dockery:
Evangelical Baptist and the Doctrine of the Bible

James Leo Garrett Jr.

INTRODUCTION[1]

A native of Tuscaloosa, Alabama, baptized at nine and ordained at twenty-eight, David Samuel Dockery is a graduate of the University of Alabama at Birmingham (B.S., 1975), Grace Theological Seminary (M.Div., 1979), Southwestern Baptist Theological Seminary (M.Div., 1981), Texas Christian University (M.A., 1985), and the University of Texas at Arlington (Ph.D., 1988). After pastoring Metropolitan Church, Brooklyn, New York (1981–1984), and teaching theology and New Testament at Criswell College, Dallas (1984–1988), he became associate professor and then professor of New Testament theology at Southern Baptist Theological Seminary (1988–1990, 1992–1996), and following a two-year period as general editor of *New American Commentary* for the Sunday School Board of the Southern Baptist Convention (now LifeWay Christian Resources), rejoined the Southern faculty, becoming dean of the School of Theology (1992–1996) and vice president of academic administration (1993–1996). In 1996 he became president

---

[1] This chapter is a slightly updated revision of the author's section on Dockery in his *Baptist Theology: A Four-Century Study* (Macon, GA: Mercer University Press, 2009), 704–11, and is published here by permission of Mercer University Press.

of Union University, Jackson, Tennessee, and professor of Christian studies and has presided over the expansion of this historic institution.[2]

Dockery has done considerable work as editor and coeditor of books. He has edited a work on the relationship of Southern Baptists to American evangelicals,[3] a book of evangelical responses to postmodernism,[4] and a *festschrift* for Millard J. Erickson.[5] He has coedited two editions of a volume interpreting Baptist theologians,[6] a *festschrift* for James Leo Garrett Jr.,[7] a volume of nineteen essays on the different methods of biblical criticism and various issues for New Testament interpretation,[8] a book consisting of divergent views of the Scriptures among Southern Baptists,[9] a comprehensive textbook on biblical hermeneutics,[10] a volume on the nature and future of Christian higher education,[11] and a volume concerning a Christian worldview for Christian higher education.[12] He was the general editor of *Holman Bible Handbook*[13] and of *Holman Concise Bible Commentary*[14] and the compiler of *The Best of A. T. Robertson*.[15] He has been a consulting editor of *Christianity Today* since 1992.

---

[2] Curriculum Vitae, Union University; *Who's Who in Religion*, 4th ed. (1992–93), 130; *Contemporary Authors* 223 (2004): 114–15.

[3] *Southern Baptists and American Evangelicals: The Conversation Continues* (Nashville: B&H, 1993).

[4] *The Challenge of Postmodernism: An Evangelical Engagement* (Grand Rapids: Baker, 1997; rev. ed., 2001).

[5] *New Dimensions in Evangelical Thought: Essays in Honor of Millard J. Erickson* (Downers Grove, IL: InterVarsity, 1998).

[6] With Timothy George, *Baptist Theologians* (Nashville: Broadman, 1990); *Theologians of the Baptist Tradition* (Nashville: B&H, 2001).

[7] With Paul A. Basden, *The People of God: Essays on the Believers' Church* (Nashville: Broadman, 1991).

[8] With David Alan Black, *New Testament Criticism and Interpretation* (Grand Rapids: Zondervan, 1991); rev. ed. titled *Interpreting the New Testament: Essays on Method and Issues* (Nashville: B&H, 2001).

[9] With Robison B. James, *Beyond the Impasse? Scripture, Interpretation, and Theology in Baptist Life* (Nashville: Broadman, 1992).

[10] With Kenneth A. Mathews and Robert B. Sloan, *Foundations for Biblical Interpretation* (Nashville: B&H, 1994).

[11] With David P. Gushee, *The Future of Christian Higher Education* (Nashville: B&H, 1999). Dockery was the author of three chapters.

[12] With Gregory Alan Thornbury, *Shaping a Christian Worldview: The Foundations of Christian Higher Education* (Nashville: B&H, 2002).

[13] Nashville: Holman Bible Publishers, 1992.

[14] Nashville: B&H, 1998.

[15] Nashville: B&H, 1996.

Dockery is the author of two commentaries (Ephesians[16] and Ecclesiastes[17]), a volume on the Sermon on the Mount (with David Garland), and a volume on Christian higher education. He is also New Testament editor of the New American Commentary series. Co-editing a fifteen-volume series, *Reclaiming the Christian Intellectual Tradition*,[18] while coauthoring one of its volumes,[19] he has also served as founding publisher of *Renewing Minds: A Journal of Christian Thought*.

SCRIPTURE AND HERMENEUTICS

Dockery's scholarly work on the doctrine of the Christian Scriptures included that which serves as prolegomena: the self-testimony of the Bible and its relationship to divine revelation and to Jesus Christ. "Both Testaments view the words of Scripture as God's own words," and Psalm 119 "exemplifies" this attitude.[20] The New Testament introduces quotations from the Old Testament by formulas such as "God says," "the Holy Spirit says," and "it is written."[21] The Old Testament prophets had employed "the word of the Lord came to me saying" and "thus says the Lord."[22] References to the need for and fact of fulfilled Old Testament prophecy are also a part of the self-testimony of the Scriptures.[23] The Bible alludes to general revelation and embodies special or particular revelation, which is progressive, personal, and propositional.[24] Jesus not only taught his disciples "that His life and ministry fulfilled the [Old Testament] Scriptures" but also provided a new Christological method of interpreting the Old Testament, that is, "in light of Himself."[25] The New Testament is a body of "Spirit-directed writings that focused on the life, ministry, death, resurrection, and exaltation of Christ."[26]

---

[16] *Ephesians: One Body in Christ* (Nashville: Convention Press, 1996).

[17] *Ecclesiastes: The Pursuit* (Nashville: LifeWay, 2011).

[18] With Timothy George (Wheaton, IL: Crossway, 2012).

[19] With Timothy George, *The Great Tradition of Christian Thinking: A Student's Guide*, vol. 1, *Reclaiming the Christian Intellectual Tradition* (Wheaton, IL: Crossway, 2012).

[20] *The Doctrine of the Bible* (Nashville: Convention Press, 1991), 41.

[21] Ibid., 42.

[22] Ibid., 44.

[23] Ibid., 46.

[24] Ibid., 12–26.

[25] Ibid., 30.

[26] Ibid., 35. See also David S. Dockery, *Christian Scripture: An Evangelical Perspective on Inspiration, Authority, and Interpretation* (Nashville: B&H, 1995), 15–35.

The Old Testament contains references to the transmission or preservation of portions of the law and the prophets, and collections of the Gospels and of the Pauline epistles existed in the second century AD.[27] "The whole Bible existed in at least seven versions [languages] . . . by the sixth century AD."[28] Dockery was agreeable to recent scholarship in positing the closure of the Old Testament canon "by the time of Jesus," if not as early as 165 BC, but he retained the traditional view that "the decisive period in the history of the New Testament canon was AD 140–200."[29]

Dockery sought to explicate "the two-sided character of the Bible as a divine-human book" so as to avoid an "ebionitic" conclusion that the Bible is only a human book and a "docetic" conclusion that it is only a divine book. Second Timothy 3:16–17 testifies to the divine inspiration of the writings, not merely the writers,[30] whereas the Bible obviously "is composed of different types of literature."[31] After defining and evaluating the dictation, illumination, encounter (Karl Barth), and dynamic theories of biblical inspiration,[32] Dockery clearly opted for the plenary theory as the one that "best accounts for the divine character of Scripture and the human circumstances of the Bible's composition."[33] Such inspired Scripture has the possibility of being both *normative* and *inerrant*.[34]

Dockery's greatest specialization has come in biblical hermeneutics, beginning with his doctoral dissertation.[35] Commencing with Jesus' Christological interpretation of the Old Testament and that of the apostles and Jewish hermeneutical methods, he traced the functional or worship-oriented interpretation by the apostolic fathers and the more authoritarian response to heresies by Irenaeus and Tertullian before contrasting the Alexandrian allegorical (Clement, Origen) method and the Antiochene literal-historical and typological (Theodore of Mopsuestia, John Chrysostom)

---

[27] See Dockery, *The Doctrine of the Bible*, 97–108.

[28] Ibid., 101.

[29] Ibid., 105–6. See also Dockery, *Christian Scripture*, 77–96.

[30] David Dockery, "The Divine-Human Authorship of Inspired Scripture," in *Authority and Interpretation: A Baptist Perspective*, ed. Duane A. Garrett and Richard R. Melick Jr. (Grand Rapids: Baker, 1987), 19–20.

[31] Ibid., 27.

[32] Ibid., 29–34.

[33] Ibid., 35.

[34] Ibid., 35–41. See also Dockery, *The Doctrine of the Bible*, 53–77, where he also refuted feminist and liberation theologies and *Christian Scripture*, 37–60.

[35] "An Examination of Hermeneutical Development in Early Christian Thought and Its Contemporary Significance" (Ph.D. diss., University of Texas at Arlington, 1988).

methods. "Canonical and Catholic hermeneutics" was represented by Jerome, Augustine of Hippo, and Theodoret of Cyrus. Dockery traced the medieval fourfold sense of Scripture to John Cassian.[36] Erasmus,[37] Calvin, and Luther were seen as the major Reformation contributors to hermeneutics, and in the post-Reformation era Protestant scholasticism employed a dogmatic hermeneutic with Aristotelian influence. Pietism produced Johann Albrecht Bengel, and rationalistic tendencies paved the way for the historical-critical method.[38] J. S. Semler's strictly historical method was followed by F. C. Baur's "tendency criticism" and the first "quest" for the historical Jesus. Dockery made a place for the "grammatical-historical exegesis" of the Princeton school and of Baptist exegetes in America.[39] He wrote in depth about John A. Broadus and A. T. Robertson.[40] Relative to contemporary hermeneutics Dockery not only surveyed the major options, namely author oriented (E. D. Hirsch), reader oriented (Hans-Georg Gadamer), and text oriented (Paul Ricoeur), but also proposed a synthesis. Accordingly, he used the text, which has "contextual keys," to bridge the "gulf" between reader and author and resurrected *sensus plenior*, or "a fuller meaning in the text than the author intended," to bring together "historical meaning" and "contemporary understanding."[41] Dockery also advocated the proper, nonabusive contemporary use of the typological method, for thereby Jesus and the apostles interpreted the Old Testament "Christologically," and therewith the unity of the two testaments can be more clearly seen.[42]

---

[36] David S. Dockery, *Biblical Interpretation Then and Now: Contemporary Hermeneutics in the Light of the Early Church* (Grand Rapids: Baker, 1992), 23–154, 158–60.

[37] David S. Dockery, "The Foundations of Reformation Hermeneutics: A Fresh Look at Erasmus," in *Evangelical Hermeneutics*, ed. Michael Bauman and David W. Hall (Camp Hill, PA: Christian Publications, 1995), 53–75.

[38] David S. Dockery, "New Testament Interpretation: A Historical Survey," in *New Testament Criticism and Interpretation*, ed. Black and Dockery, 47–50; also in *Interpreting the New Testament*, ed. Black and Dockery, 26–28. See also "The History of Pre-Critical Biblical Interpretation," *Faith and Mission* 10 (Fall 1992): 3–33.

[39] David S. Dockery, "New Testament Interpretation: A Historical Survey," in *Interpreting the New Testament*, ed. Black and Dockery, 28–34.

[40] David S. Dockery, "John Albert Broadus," in *Bible Interpreters of the Twentieth Century*, ed. Elwell and Powell, 37–49; David S. Dockery, "The Broadus-Robertson Tradition," in *Theologians of the Baptist Tradition*, ed. George and Dockery, 90–114.

[41] David S. Dockery, "Author? Reader? Text? Toward a Hermeneutical Synthesis," *Theological Educator* 38 (1988): 7–16; Dockery, *Biblical Interpretation Then and Now*, 168–83.

[42] David S. Dockery, "Typological Exegesis: Moving Beyond Abuse and Neglect," in *Reclaiming the Prophetic Mantle: Preaching the Old Testament Faithfully*, ed. George L. Klein (Nashville: Broadman, 1992), 161–78, esp. 162–63, 174–75. With George H. Guthrie

NAVIGATING DIFFICULT DOCTRINES AND
DENOMINATIONAL CONTROVERSY

Dockery was deeply involved in the more reflective aspects of the SBC inerrancy controversy. He began in 1985 by affirming a "critical inerrancy" view of the autographs "not only in matters of salvation, but in all matters of ethics and issues of life."[43] Then he defined and explained seven different views of biblical inerrancy and two of noninerrancy as espoused by various recent evangelical authors and concluded that there was something to be learned from most of the views about inerrancy.[44] In 1988, he differentiated four groups of Southern Baptists in respect to the question of biblical inerrancy (fundamentalists, evangelicals, moderates, and liberals) and concluded that evangelicals and moderates were more numerous. He noted that inerrancy had been erroneously identified with the mechanical dictation theory and with a strictly literal interpretation of the Bible. He called for the recognition of "the mystery of inspiration" and the use of canonical criticism and asserted that inerrancy is "the proper implication of the result of scripture's inspiration."[45] The same year he refuted Gordon James's *Inerrancy in the Southern Baptist Convention*.[46] Later, after the subsiding of the most heated controversy, the Union president reflected on the views of the Scriptures held by James P. Boyce, Basil Manly Jr., B. H. Carroll, E. Y. Mullins, and W. T. Conner; reviewed Southern Baptist theological development from 1952 to 1979 and the subsequent controversy; and restated biblical inerrancy with a view toward a more complete "evangelical orthodox consensus."[47] Recently Dockery proposed a way forward for Southern Baptists by reclaiming the Baptist heritage.[48]

---

he coauthored a handbook for lay readers: *The Holman Guide to Interpreting the Bible* (Nashville: B&H, 2004).

[43] David S. Dockery, "Can Baptists Affirm the Reliability and Authority of the Bible?," *SBC Today* 2 (March 1985): 16.

[44] David S. Dockery, "Variations on Inerrancy," *SBC Today* 4 (May 1986): 10–11.

[45] David S. Dockery, "Biblical Inerrancy: Pro or Con?" *Theological Educator* 37 (1988): 15–36 (esp. 22–24).

[46] (Dallas: Southern Baptist Heritage Press, 1986). David S. Dockery, "On Houses on Sand, Holy Wars and Heresies: A Review of the Inerrancy Controversy in the SBC," *Criswell Theological Review* 2 (Spring 1988): 391–401.

[47] David S. Dockery, "The Crisis of Scripture in Southern Baptist Life: Reflections on the Past, Looking to the Future," *Southern Baptist Journal of Theology* 9 (Spring 2005): 36–53.

[48] David S. Dockery, *Southern Baptist Consensus and Renewal: A Biblical, Historical, and Theological Proposal* (Nashville: B&H, 2008).

Dockery did not hold to a strict *sola Scriptura* position inasmuch as he emphasized the role of confessions of faith as "secondary or tertiary."[49] Furthermore he was confident Baptists needed to retain and reaffirm the patristic orthodoxy relative to the Trinity and Christology.[50] On soteriology he has espoused a Calminian or Amyraldian position between Calvinism and Arminianism—which Roger E. Olson has declared impossible.[51] He holds to unlimited atonement and affirms that "the convicting grace of God's Spirit can be rejected." "God is the sole efficient cause of salvation," but "there are also secondary and tertiary causes."[52] Faith is both "altogether brought about by God" and "altogether the human response."[53]

Dockery's writing on baptism has focused on the New Testament testimony rather than historic Baptist or contemporary issues.[54] Yet on the Lord's Supper he has strongly advocated going beyond a "memorial-only" view by recovering the spiritual presence of Christ as affirmed by the Second London Confession and more frequent observance following self-examination and in the context of worship.[55]

Regarding eschatology, writing at the turn of the twenty-first century for Baptist church members, Dockery stressed the eschatological aspect of the kingdom of God.[56] In his review of mistaken expectations of the kingdom throughout church history, he affirmed both physical and spiritual death as the penal consequence of sin, held to an intermediate state, and critiqued

---

[49] David S. Dockery, "Herschel H. Hobbs," in *Theologians of the Baptist Tradition*, ed. Timothy George and David Dockery, rev. ed. (Nashville: B&H, 2001), 221–22.

[50] David S. Dockery, "Blending Baptist with Orthodox in the Christian University," in *The Future of Baptist Higher Education*, ed. Donald D. Schmeltekopf and Dianna Vitzana (Waco, TX: Baylor University Press, 2006), 83–97, esp. 87–88.

[51] David S. Dockery, *Arminian Theology: Myths and Realities* (Downers Grove, IL: InterVarsity, 2006), 61–77.

[52] David S. Dockery, *The Gospel of Jesus Christ: By Grace Through Faith* (Jackson, TN: Union University, 2004).

[53] David S. Dockery, *Basic Christian Beliefs*, Shepherd's Notes; Bible Summary Series (Nashville: B&H, 2000), 52.

[54] David S. Dockery, "Baptism," in *Dictionary of Jesus and the Gospels*, ed. Joel B. Green and Scot McKnight (Downers Grove, IL; Leicester UK: InterVarsity, 1992), 55–58; David S. Dockery, "Baptism in the New Testament," *Southwestern Journal of Theology* 43 (Spring 2001): 4–16.

[55] David S. Dockery, "The Lord's Supper in the New Testament and in Baptist Worship," *Search* 19 (Fall 1988): 38–48.

[56] But Dockery and David E. Garland held that the Sermon on the Mount is presently "obligatory on all citizens of the kingdom." *Seeking the Kingdom: The Sermon on the Mount Made Practical for Today* (Wheaton, IL: Harold Shaw, 1992), 9.

reincarnation. After reviewing the various millennial views, he opted for historic premillennialism of the posttribulational type. He affirmed final judgment, hell, and heaven, refuting annihilationism and universalism in support of an exclusivism relative to the unevangelized.[57]

CONCLUSION

More than any other theologian Dockery has fleshed out anew the doctrine of the Bible during, after, and on behalf of the conservative resurgence in the Southern Baptist Convention. Exploring the self-testimony of the Bible and following recent Old Testament scholarship as to the earlier closing of the Old Testament canon, he affirmed the Bible as a divine-human book whose divine inspiration is best served by the plenary theory. Analyzing numerous views of biblical inerrancy, Dockery espoused "critical inerrancy." He traced the history of biblical hermeneutics from the early church through the late twentieth century and advocated a text-oriented approach with use of *sensus plenior*, typology, and canonical criticism. Not embracing a strict *sola Scriptura* position, the Union president held to the secondary authority of confessions of faith and to patristic orthodoxy as to the Trinity and Christology. Taking a Calminian or Amyraldian stance on the doctrine of salvation, Dockery has more recently led in seeking to prevent strife or schism among Southern Baptists over Calvinist-Arminian issues.[58]

---

[57] David S. Dockery, *Our Christian Hope* (Nashville: LifeWay, 1998), 8–24, 28–29, 35–38, 42–43, 67–85, 92–126. See also Dockery, *Basic Christian Beliefs*, 79–88.

[58] Dockery served as chairman of the Calvinism Advisory Committee appointed by the president of the Southern Baptist Convention's Executive Committee (2012–13).

With David Dockery Among
Baptists and Evangelicals

Timothy George

*Think where man's glory most begins and ends,
and say my glory was that I had such
friends.—William Butler Yeats*

Enduring friendships can begin in strange places. My friendship with David S. Dockery began in a cemetery, the famous Cave Hill Cemetery in Louisville. Cave Hill is a beautiful, leafy, urban cemetery adjacent to the Southern Baptist Theological Seminary where, in the summer of 1987, I was about to begin my tenth year as a member of the faculty. David was a professor at the Criswell College in Dallas and had been invited by seminary president Roy L. Honeycutt to teach a summer course at Southern in fulfillment of the pledge recently made by the six SBC seminary presidents to add scholarly conservative voices to their faculties and curricula.

I often took my students on "field trips" to Cave Hill Cemetery. Some of the great figures in Baptist history lie buried there, including James P. Boyce, the founder of Southern Seminary, and John A. Broadus, his close friend and colleague. One of the most impressive gravesites was that of the famous New Testament scholar, A. T. Robertson, marked by a simple white stone inscribed with the words of Philippians 1:21, "To me to live is Christ and to die is gain." Cave Hill Cemetery had become a sacred place to me during my years in Louisville, and I wanted to introduce it to my new friend, David Dockery.

As we walked together through beautiful Cave Hill Cemetery on that warm summer afternoon in 1987, we discussed many things including the debt each of us felt to the rich theological legacy of those great theologians and church leaders above whose mortal remains we stood. Some of them, along with their predecessors and peers, were hardly remembered anymore, or if they were, they were merely names from long ago, relegated to the realm of affectionate obscurity. The story of their faith, courage, and commitment to the church of Jesus Christ—all this a distant memory. David and I determined to collect a volume of essays which we hoped would be an introduction to the life and thought of some of the most notable shapers of Baptist theology. Our book, *Baptist Theologians* (1990), a volume of 704 pages with thirty-five chapters, treated Baptist theologians from John Bunyan to Clark Pinnock. We dedicated *Baptist Theologians* to the two pastors who had ordained us to the gospel ministry, J. Ralph McIntyre (Timothy) and Darold H. Morgan (David).

Although we did not know it at the time, the summer of 1987 marked a major transition in both of our lives. One year later David would be moving to Louisville to become a full-time member of the faculty and later dean of Southern's School of Theology and vice president for academic administration. In the meantime I had received a call from President Thomas E. Corts of Samford University inviting me to consider becoming the founding dean of a new institution of theological education, soon to be named Beeson Divinity School. So David and I passed like ships in the night that year, he moving from Dallas to Louisville and I from Louisville to Birmingham.

Birmingham was the hometown of both David and his wife Lanese, and their parents were still living there at the time. David and I had many occasions to see each other in Alabama and elsewhere, often over some good Mexican food. Our personal friendship had emerged through our tentative efforts to reach out to each other across the boundaries of divergence which had placed us (without asking us) on opposite sides of the polemical divide in what was then a raging denominational quarrel. In the process a marvelous thing happened: We experienced a mutual conversion as we discovered a surprising confluence of ideas and commitments, not only between the two of us but also among a wider circle of colleagues and friends. Through correspondence and conversation, through times of prayer and fellowship, we came to see that we had far more in common than the stereotypes others had used to describe where we "belonged" in this camp or that.

While fulfilling demanding administrative responsibilities in our respective institutions, we both continued to do research, to write, and to publish in our respective fields, Reformation studies for me and biblical interpretation for David. We contributed articles to each other's projects, read each other's books and, when asked, offered endorsements to each other's publishers. Beyond these specifics we also shared what might be called a common "project" driven by a "common spirit," one that went back to our conversation and that walk through Cave Hill Cemetery in 1987. In the preface to the first edition of our first coedited book, we described this approach—actually our dreams—in this way.

> We desire to foster a forum where scholars from diverse perspectives within the Baptist family could share the results of their research and in the process experience, perhaps, the miracle of dialogue—not a raucous shouting at one another, nor a snide whispering behind each other's backs, but a genuine listening and learning in the context of humane inquiry and disciplined thought. . . . In our search for common ground, we do not declare theological neutrality. We rejoice in the renewed commitment to biblical faith within our own denomination, as well as in reports of evangelical awakening among Baptists throughout the world. However, such movings of the Spirit, if they are not to degenerate into shallow piosity, must also be accompanied by theological revival. The Christian faith is deeper and wider than the spiritual experience of any one believer: it is the confession of Jesus Christ as Lord, and the living out of that confession by the power of the Holy Spirit in the midst of the people of God. Theology is not an ivory-tower exercise for stuffy academics: it is the serious responsibility of every Christian and every church that seeks to be faithful to its Lord. By seeing how others before us have articulated the faith, we will be better able to formulate a proper theology for our own turbulent times.

During the 1990s and continuing into the new millennium, these aspirations found expression primarily in two major arenas: the Baptist tradition we both loved and belonged to, and the wider evangelical community we understood ourselves to be a part of. In a time of widening denominational conflict in the SBC, both David and I believed it was important for those who held different views and who found themselves in different denominational camps to speak directly with one another face-to-face, to pray together as brothers and sisters in Christ, and to explore serious theological differences in an attitude of charity and humility.

While many factors, including politics and personalities, had fueled the SBC controversy, the nature of the Bible and its authority were at the heart of the dispute. In 1991, David was asked to write the doctrine study book for the Southern Baptist Convention on *The Doctrine of the Bible*. David approached the hot-wire issue of biblical inerrancy with thoughtful analysis, careful definition, and interpretive savvy. Later this book was expanded into a major publication called *Christian Scripture* (1995). This is only one of many books David has devoted to the theme of the Bible over the course of his career. James Leo Garrett, one of David's mentors, has noted that "David S. Dockery has written more about the nature and interpretation of the Bible than any other Southern Baptist theologian in history."

David Dockery has spent a great deal of time building bridges, or trying to build bridges, over chasms seemingly too wide to span. One such project in which David and I were both involved from 1989 until 1992 was called "Beyond the Impasse." We were joined by six other Baptist scholars who met on several occasions for a series of discussions related to the implosion of our denominational fellowship at the time. In addition to David and me, the other members of the team included Walter Harrelson, John P. Newport, R. Albert Mohler, Robison B. James, Paige Patterson, and Molly Truman Marshall. The eight of us were a diverse lot, representing a wide span of differences among Southern Baptists at the time. Several moderate Baptist groupings, including the Alliance of Baptists and the Cooperative Baptist Fellowship, had already taken initial steps to form their own organizations separate from the Southern Baptist Convention. Our dialogue project was in a sense the last-ditch attempt to stay the centrifugal forces pulling the denomination apart. Our discussions were marked by candor, civility, and some drama, for we all knew how high the stakes were. On one occasion I recall one member of our team breaking down in tears at the prospect of our denominational divorce. This experiment in reconciliation was a worthy effort, and I am glad we tried, but at the end of the day we failed. When the papers from this project were finally published, we found it necessary to add a question mark to the title, *Beyond the Impasse? Scripture, Interpretation, and Theology in Baptist Life* (1992).

More than anyone I can think of in recent decades, David Dockery has fulfilled the role of denominational statesman among Southern Baptists. The departure of many Baptist moderates from SBC denominational life during the 1990s has not resulted in placid waters or stormless seas among the Baptist majority that remained intact. Several years ago David and I wrote a little book, *Building Bridges*, which called for the renewal of consensus and cooperation for Southern Baptists in the twenty-first century. This book was published by the executive committee of the Southern Baptist Convention and distributed to every registered messenger at the annual SBC meeting in 2007. More recently I was pleased to serve with David and other leaders on the SBC Calvinism Advisory Committee. This was an effort initiated by Dr. Frank Page, president of the SBC executive committee, to come to greater mutual understanding and to find a way forward over the increasingly contentious issue of Calvinism. Our group issued a report titled "Truth, Trust and Testimony in a Time of Tension: A Statement from the Calvinism Advisory Committee," which was accepted and affirmed by the SBC at its annual meeting in Houston in 2013. David was the quiet leader of our group, and Frank Page was wise to ask him to help coordinate our work.

Having observed David at work over the years in a number of mediating efforts such as this one, I think I know why he is so effective. First, he listens superbly well. Beneath his low-key, apparently shy demeanor, deep thoughts are always churning, and a possible strategy for moving forward is emerging. But David never rushes in with "ten ideas I must get on the table before anyone else speaks." He takes his time, slowly, deliberately, patiently listening to everyone's ideas and learning from what they say. Then when he does speak, we listen.

Second, David weds together conciliation and conviction. It would be a big mistake to confuse David's natural modesty and soft-spokenness with timidity or wishy-washiness. David is a person of deep Christian conviction, hard-won beliefs forged on the anvil of God's unshakeable Word and tested in the crucible of conflict and temptation. But he knows that the Master's preferred way of entering the human heart is to beckon, not bludgeon (cf. Rev 3:20). The way of conciliation is the way of Christ, and, coincidentally, it is almost always the way of getting better results.

And, finally, David has the remarkable ability of saying just enough but not too much. Once when someone had written me a letter demanding that I respond to a controversial issue in the news, I asked David's advice, and he reminded me that I had no obligation to respond to every question I was asked. David Dockery has learned well the lesson of Proverbs 25:11, "A word spoken at the right time is like gold apples on a silver tray."

Are Southern Baptists evangelicals? What hath Nashville to do with Wheaton? These questions formed an important subtext during the SBC controversy. In 1983, noted scholars James Leo Garrett and E. Glenn Hinson engaged in a thoughtful exchange on this issue, which resulted in the book, *Are Southern Baptists Evangelicals?* (1982). Garrett's answer was basically affirmative, while Hinson's was definitely negative. During this time Foy Valentine, an SBC agency head, expressed his own views on the subject in words that have often been quoted. In a fit of Baptist braggadocio, he said: "We are not evangelicals. That's a Yankee word. They want to claim us because we are big and successful and growing every year. But we have our own traditions, our own hymns and more students in our seminaries than they have in all of theirs put together."[1]

Although Hinson and Valentine were decidedly on the moderate side of the Baptist squabble, the question itself did not break down into a pure party-line distinction. For example, Garrett was a member of the moderate/liberal Broadway Baptist Church in Fort Worth (whose history he later wrote) and can in no sense be counted as a partisan within the conservative turnaround/takeover movement. Likewise, some ultraconservative Baptists resented any notion of an SBC-evangelical coziness as much as Foy Valentine seemed to. The fact is that from the 1920s through the 1980s, the Mason-Dixon invisible wall between North and South had grown stronger, not weaker. It served to reinforce a sense of Baptist identity that assumed self-sufficiency, denominational autonomy, and the need to construct and protect the Southern Baptist Zion from contamination.

This neo-isolationist spirit prevailed at both ends of the SBC spectrum. On the part of those few moderates who showed any interest in Christian unity, it was largely a one-way-to-the-left ecumenism they pursued. For example, Southern Seminary hosted a consultation of the World Council of Churches on its campus in 1979 while refusing to invite to campus noted evangelical scholars such as Carl F. H. Henry, J. I. Packer, and Kenneth Kantzer. On the other side of the fence, the "we're just fine; we don't need anybody else"

---

[1] Foy Valentine, quoted by Kenneth L. Woodard in "Born Again! The Year of the Evangelicals," *Newsweek* 88 (October 25, 1976): 76. The issue of whether Southern Baptists were evangelicals was classically discussed in two books a decade apart as the SBC moved through the conservative resurgence: James Leo Garrett Jr., E. Glenn Hinson, and James E. Tull, eds., *Are Southern Baptists "Evangelicals"?* (Macon: Mercer University Press, 1983), and David Dockery, ed. (including contributions by Garrett and Hinson), *Southern Baptists and American Evangelicals: The Conversation Continues* (Nashville: B&H, 1993).

attitude was a natural fit for those Southern Baptists still shaped by, and harking back to, the Landmarkist impulse of the nineteenth and early twentieth centuries.

One of the things that drew David and me together in the early days of our friendship was a clear sense that this dichotomy was unhealthy, unnecessary, and based on a fallacious reading of Baptist history. It seemed obvious to us that, of course, Southern Baptists were evangelicals—admittedly evangelicals with their own Southern-fried distinctives, one of which was the very denominational cocooning that downplayed their affinity with other like-minded evangelical believers. Prior to the fundamentalist-modernist conflicts of the 1920s and 1930s, there had been robust two-way traffic across the Mason-Dixon Line. The great John A. Broadus frequently preached in northern pulpits, and Southern Seminary's first academic building, New York Hall, was so called because of supporters from that state, including the Rockefeller family.

In any event, our sense of how Southern Baptists fit into the wider scheme of things was reinforced by David Bebbington's famous evangelical quadrilateral which first appeared in his 1989 book, *Evangelicalism in Modern Britain: A History from the 1730s to the 1980s*. There Bebbington, a Scottish Baptist, described four defining characteristics that marked evangelicals in general: a solid commitment to the Bible and its authority; a focus on Jesus Christ and his sacrificial death on the cross; teaching about the necessity of conversion, the new birth; and an activism evident in the world-encompassing missionary movement. If Bebbington had been trying to characterize Southern Baptists at the time, he could hardly have found four more applicable, well-fitting traits. With this in mind, David and I included in the first edition of *Baptist Theologians* not only great Baptist figures from the past and some contemporary Southern Baptist theologians but also a number of figures whose work and ministry was largely carried out beyond the bounds of the SBC. These included George Eldon Ladd, Millard J. Erickson, James Deotis Roberts, Edward John Carnell, Bernard Ramm, George R. Beasley-Murray, Carl F. H. Henry, and Clark H. Pinnock.

Over the past quarter century, both David and I have continued to promote, in our writings and activities, greater mutuality and intentional reciprocity between the Baptist community and the wider evangelical world. During these years David has emerged not only as a denominational statesman within the Tennessee Baptist Convention and the Southern Baptist Convention but also as a highly esteemed servant-leader among extra-SBC evangelicals as well. His contributions in this arena include service on the boards of *Christianity Today*, Prison Fellowship Ministries (a position for which he was recommended by Chuck Colson), the Manhattan Declaration, and the American Academy of Ministry. He has also served on the board of the Council for Christian Colleges and Universities, including a term of service as board chair. While his transformative work as the fifteenth president of Union University has come to a close, David Dockery's visionary leadership within the Baptist family and within the greater evangelical community will, let us pray, continue unabated for many years to come. The same is true for his prolific work as a scholar and writer, with new publications now in the press and many others yet to come.

In this brief essay I have written about my friendship with David Dockery and our partnership in various scholarly, academic, and church-related endeavors. I want to close with a personal word. Over the many years I have known David Dockery, the great respect and esteem in which I hold him have only increased. We have been fellow travelers and fellow pilgrims. We have laughed together, cried together, and dreamed together. We have sought each other's counsel when facing important decisions in our lives. We have prayed together for each other's families and about many other matters both great and small. His work at Union University has been remarkable and will bear good fruit for many generations to come. His unswerving commitment to Jesus Christ and to his church have encouraged me, perhaps more than he knows. At this milestone in his life, I salute my dear friend and wish him the speed of God as he gears up for the journey yet to come.

Toward Convictional Civility

Millard J. Erickson

INTRODUCTION

The theme of convictional civility is an appropriate one for the title of a book honoring David Dockery, for to an unusual degree he has embodied, in his person and in his professional roles, deeply held convictions, expressed with civility and courtesy. While the church's only model and standard is its Lord, it benefits from the example of faithful servants of Jesus Christ, who in their lives reflect the grace of that Lord and Savior. The church today might well look to Dockery as a guide in the manner of its conduct today. This is especially important in our time, for certain cultural forces constitute a challenge to that combination of conviction and civility.

Although the church is not to be of the world, it must inevitably, if it is to be the church faithfully, be involved in that world. An understanding of the cultural milieu can, therefore, both help us understand the situation into which the church is to proclaim and live the gospel and avoid its becoming conformed to the world. Such areas of human activity as commerce, art, and politics may give a clue.

CIVILITY

One obstacle to civility today is the polarization present in American society. This can perhaps be seen most clearly in the realm of politics. While this is sometimes depicted anecdotally as the extremes of the Tea Party on the right and virtual socialism on the left, it is pervasive and represents a considerable shift from an earlier period. This shift can be documented from the voting records of the members of Congress over the years, assuming the traditional depiction of the Republican Party as more conservative and the Democratic Party as more liberal. In 1982, the most liberal Republican senator, according to this rating method, was Lowell Weicker of Connecticut, and the most conservative Democratic senator was Edward Zorinsky of Nebraska. Between the two lay twenty-three Republicans and thirty-five Democrats. By 1994, only eight Republicans and twenty-six Democrats had voting records that fell between those of the most liberal Republican, James Jeffords of Vermont, and the most conservative Democrat, Richard Shelby of Alabama. By 2002, only six Republicans and one Democrat fell into the overlap; and by 2010, no senator of either party had this sort of mediating voting record.[1] In the House of Representatives, a similar pattern could be found, with members with middle-ground voting records declining from 344 in 1982, to 226 in 1999, 54 in 2005, and only 7 in 2010.[2]

Some of this can be explained by citizens' voting patterns and shifting party allegiances by members of Congress, rather than changes in voting by representatives and senators. So, for example, the "Blue Dog" Democrats, who were moderate or even conservative in their views, generally represented conservative districts, whose voters then elected Republicans in their place; but that in itself is a significant indicator. Several conservative Democrats, often from the South, switched parties, as did liberal Republicans. The change in voting patterns has in recent years been accompanied by a greater rigidity of position, with the Republican minority leader of the Senate declaring that the major goal of his party was to prevent the reelection of President Obama, and the president declaring that he would not negotiate with the House Republicans on the budget. The tone of the rhetoric has also become elevated.

It appears at times that completely different worldviews are involved. One commentator observed that for liberals (or as some often now term themselves, "progressives") global warming is the dominant issue, while for

---

[1]   Peter Bell, Scott Gland, and Ryan Morris, "Toeing the Line," *National Journal*, February 24, 2011, accessed July 7, 2014, http://www.nationaljournal.com/magazine/vote-ratings-senate-centrists-in-decline-20110224.

[2]   Ronald Brownstein, "Pulling Apart," *National Journal*, February 24, 2011, accessed July 7, 2014, http://www.nationaljournal.com/magazine/congress-hits-new-peak-in-polarization-20110224.

conservatives it is international terrorism. The same could be said of income inequality and the national debt. Some of these issues, such as same-sex marriage and abortion, are so emotionally charged that there not only is no middle ground, but there is a tendency to demonize those who differ.

A similar polarization can be found in matters of religion. On a global scale the conflict between Islam and several other religions has produced violent results in numerous cases. For example, in predominantly Muslim countries, attacks by Muslims on Christians appear to be multiplying, and in some cases Hindus are also being targeted. Violence between Shiite and Sunni Muslims is frequent. Even within Christian circles there is a large gap between liberals, whose concerns often run to social problems, including gay rights, and evangelicals, whose primary orientation is to evangelism. Among the latter, disputes sometimes have been acrimonious. Even among evangelicals, the middle ground is not a comfortable place to stand, for one receives fire from both sides. One evangelical theologian said of the Evangelical Theological Society, "In this organization we have medievalists and postmodernists, and nothing in between." Although that was a bit of an overstatement, there is considerable basis to what he said.

In addition to this polarization, there are a number of other obstacles to civility.

1. Attempts to suppress expression of differing opinions. In an earlier period the ideal, at least in academic settings, was for the free expression of ideas in the intellectual marketplace, so that each viewpoint could be argued for and persons could draw their own conclusions and incorporate those into their convictions. In our postmodern milieu, however, sometimes what Stanley Fish has termed persuasion rather than demonstration takes place. In the latter, one assumed there were objective facts and neutral positions from which these could be examined and evaluated. In the former, however, one simply shares what one sees from one's own perspective and invites others to accept this.[3] What this involves is attempting to persuade one to join one's interpretive community, and the determining factor becomes the skill of the speaker or writer. In practice, however, this has a tendency to lead to subjective or even coercive activity. As long ago as 1987, Alan Bloom described the relativism that came to be known as political correctness.[4] In such a situation, only

---

[3] Stanley Fish, *Is There a Text in This Class? The Authority of Interpretive Communities* (Cambridge, MA: Harvard University Press, 1980), 365.

[4] Allan Bloom, *The Closing of the American Mind: How Higher Education Has Failed Democracy and Impoverished the Souls of Today's Students* (New York: Simon & Schuster, 1987).

one viewpoint has the right to be heard, and so steps are taken to prevent the hearing of differing perspectives.

Sometimes at public addresses those who oppose the viewpoint of the speaker create such a disturbance that the speaker's words are drowned out. In short, an attempt is made to prevent those ideas from even being heard, let alone considered and possibly adopted. The ultimate form of this is the pie in the face where the speaker is not only silenced but humiliated publicly. This is a considerable departure from the ideal once embodied in institutions of education, of allowing the free expression of ideas, and the right for these to compete in the marketplace of ideas. Indeed, this was one of the values that led the framers of the United States Constitution to include the First Amendment.

These are examples of incivility. They involve disrespect for the other person and are reflected in inattention to the other's expressions, *ad hominem* references, flat rejection of the other's ideas, and often misrepresentation of those ideas. Unfortunately Christians have not always avoided such problems, and the temptations are especially severe today.

2. *Insincere use of the term and concept of civility.* By this I mean accusing the other person of incivility while engaging in uncivil activity oneself. The conventional account is that conservatives—or as sometimes labeled, fundamentalists—have been cranky, mean, narrow-minded, unreasonable, and unfair. In the fundamentalist-modernist controversy, this charge was frequently leveled against fundamentalists.

> The fundamentalists lost their battle [for the denominations] for the lack of a few elemental things. The first of these was courtesy. They sought to bowl over their opponents by the very boisterousness of their attack. Culling choice epithets from the language of popular evangelists, they called names which made the mob laugh, but which hurt all believers in Christ.[5]

It should be noted, however, that such discourtesy was not the exclusive possession of the fundamentalists. Plenty of examples of a lack of courtesy by conservatives could be cited. Two years after the publication of the quotation cited above, the editor of the journal in which it appeared wrote the following:

> But in his efforts to secure practical control at Princeton—as well as

---

5 "The Retreating Wave of Fundamentalism," *Christian Century* 40, no. 25 (June 21, 1923): 771.

in his efforts to promote the fundamentalist program in the Presbyterian denomination at large—Dr. Machen has revealed a capacity for detailed maneuverings, an aptitude for political finesse, together with a rigidity of mind and spirit that have made him feared more than admired. Son of a conservative Maryland family—he has one brother who heads the movement in that state for the repeal of the 18th amendment to the federal constitution—Dr. Machen reveals the antipathy to change of any kind which characterizes that section of society. As he sits brooding in an assembly, dark eye-brows drawn down across a dark face, he looks every inch the man who instinctively votes "no" on any proposal involving change. One suspects that he suffers with his digestion. He is not married.[6]

We should be aware that there has been a revival of what must at least be termed a paradoxical appeal to civility or ironic irenicism in our time. In one denomination two groups debated a doctrinal position, or at least the right to hold and teach it at a denominational school. The less conservative group included "Committed to Civility" in its name. Yet many in the more conservative group testified that they had never experienced less civility than the treatment they received at the hands of the "civility" group.[7] In another case one theologian, whose view was under criticism, seemed to imply that to criticize his view was unloving. The admonition to civility needs to be observed by all parties to discussion.[8]

Journalism, in the broad sense, also reveals a lack of respect for others with whom one differs. One genre of television broadcasting that has grown in popularity is the talk-show format, in which a number of panelists interact on a given subject or subjects. At one time these were civil in nature, with each person patiently waiting his or her turn to speak and disagreeing while at least acknowledging the other person's position and the possible validity of some of those thoughts expressed. Now, however, it is not uncommon for two or more speakers to speak simultaneously, each speaking over the other. Even when one is not speaking, it is apparent that he or she is not really listening to

---

[6] Paul Hutchinson, "The Battle of Princeton—1925," ibid., XLII.22 (May 28, 1925): 699.

[7] In the interests of the desired civility, specific identification and documentation will be omitted in any references to contemporary persons and groups other than those who have openly identified with the ideas or characteristics under discussion.

[8] Arthur C. Brooks has documented the contention that, contrary to public opinion, American political liberals tend to be more hostile toward conservatives than vice versa: "Liberal Hatemongers," *Wall Street Journal*, January 17, 2008, A6.

and considering the view being expressed but is simply thinking about what to say next.

3. *The decline of courtesy and consideration in our society.* The expressions "thank you" and "you're welcome" have been replaced for some younger persons by "there you go" and "no problem," respectively. "You guys" has replaced "sir" or "madam," except by Southerners or members of the military. Translated into discourse, this can result in disregard for the needs and rights of others and disrespect for them as persons.

CONVICTION

A key concept in the issue is the adjective "convictional." Our age is one in which tolerance is important. It is acceptable to hold personal beliefs, but the problem comes when one attempts to convince others of the truth of these convictions. Pluralism is the idea that there may be more than one true view on a given issue. Thus, Christianity is true for Christians, but Islam is true for Muslims, and Hinduism is true for Hindus. This pluralism in turn may have several varieties. One is the idea that truth is merely a functional matter.[9] For Hindus, Hinduism enables Hindus to adjust adequately to life and to function successfully and even happily, while Shintoism serves similarly for Shintoists. A second variety says that our traditions shape the reality we find. Thus, the traditional Christian perceives the world as theistic while the Hindu sees it as pantheistic.[10] Either way, there is no point in trying to convince the other of one's own viewpoint because beliefs are not reproductions of objective reality. In such a situation, attempting to convince the other of one's view is considered intolerant or an insult to the other person. In terms of the present discussion, it is considered uncivil.

While there is not space to argue it within the context of this chapter, I contend that the kind of conviction that would be acceptable in such a context really should not be called a conviction at all. For one of two things would then be true of such a belief. The first is that it is not really a belief in the sense of being an intellectual matter. It is more an attitudinal matter. The person holding it feels better because of believing it is true. In this respect the logical positivists were correct. The second possibility, however, is that the content of the belief is not really what it appears to be. Rather than the belief

---

[9]   Richard Rorty, *Contingency, Irony, and Solidarity* (Cambridge: Cambridge University Press, 1989), 7–9.

[10] John Hick, *God Has Many Names* (London: Macmillan, 1980), 104–9.

being, "This conception is true," it should be stated, "This is one of several true alternatives on this issue." The former is the subjectivist version while the latter is the pluralist version. In the first case it is an attitude. In the second case it is a meta-conviction, or a conviction about the nature and interrelationship of specific convictions. So, in this essay, by "conviction" we mean holding that a particular proposition is true, that is, that it correctly describes a state of affairs whose existence is independent of the knower or believer considering it to be true.[11]

In one sense it is easy to be civil if no convictions, in the sense defined above, are involved, for there really cannot be any substantive disagreement. Thus there will be no attempt to get the other person to change his/her mind or allegiance. Consequently, there is a much-reduced chance for conflict and, with it, potential incivility. With tolerance comes civility most of the time.

Yet that answer may be misleading. For is tolerance really civil in the broadest sense of civility? If there is objective truth, then if I fail to tell another of that truth, especially if it involves a crucial, perhaps even a life-and-death, issue, am I really showing love to that person? Tolerance, simply saying, "I'll let him believe whatever he wants to believe," may be merely a matter of indifference to the person, of not caring about him or her. Eleanor Roosevelt is alleged to have once said, "Tolerance is an ugly word," meaning this very thing.

There is, however, an interesting contrast to this question. We noted earlier the strong political polarization within this country, and one might assume this is based on different convictions. Thus, persons are Democrats and display a more liberal voting pattern because their basic beliefs or convictions are more liberal, while Republicans vote more conservatively because their beliefs are more conservative. So, for example, a 2010 Harris poll asked U.S. adults whether Barack Obama was born in the United States. Forty-five percent of Republicans responded that he had been born outside the United States, but only 8 percent of Democrats did.[12] This same sort of divide between Republicans and Democrats appears in many other similar studies.

---

[11] This expresses the view of truth known as the correspondence theory of truth. I have argued that on the prereflective or practical level everyone assumes this conception of truth (*Truth or Consequences: The Promise and Perils of Postmodernism* [Downers Grove, IL: InterVarsity, 2001], 234–37).

[12] Harris Interactive, March 24, 2010, "'Wingnuts' and President Obama," accessed July 7, 2014, http://www.harrisinteractive.com/NewsRoom/HarrisPolls/tabid/447/ctl/Read Custom%20Default/mid/1508/ArticleId/223/Default.aspx.

Two recent studies shed a different light on this contention, however. In each study all participants were given a set of factual questions, but some were told that they would receive a financial incentive for giving the correct answer. The latter group showed significantly lower partisan differences, the average across all questions posed being about 55–60 percent. In the second study another variable was introduced, in which an incentive was also given for admitting that they did not know the correct response. Under these conditions the partisan gap was reduced even further, about 80 percent less than when no incentives were offered.[13]

A number of inferences could be drawn from these studies. One is that people sometimes express stronger views than they actually hold. These studies also suggest that the forces of social pressure or at least social cohesion play a larger part in the formation of a person's expressed views than has formerly been thought. Further, we might infer that political polarization in the United States is less than sometimes believed. Perhaps most encouraging of all is the possibility that polarization can be reduced under the right circumstances. This is particularly the case with those whose change was related to the search for accuracy rather than declared uncertainty since the latter might indicate uncertainty simply to get the reward—something that could not as easily be done in attempting to give the correct answer. A practical application of this study is that progress can be made toward agreement if persons can be led to see the general point that knowing and acting on the truth is to their advantage.

STEPS TOWARD CONVICTIONAL CIVILITY

If our goal is convictional civility, are there steps that we may take to make progress toward that goal? I suggest some that may be helpful:

1. Develop self-understanding. The ancient Greeks urged this upon their disciples, and it is still a worthwhile endeavor. In recent years we have heard much about the conditioned nature of our knowledge. Postmodernists in particular have emphasized that we never really know the world from a "God's-eye perspective." All our knowledge is from within the limitations of our situation temporally, culturally, linguistically. Indeed, who we are shapes what we know and how we know it. This was not an original discovery by

---

[13] John G. Bullock, Alan S. Gerber, Seth J. Hill, and Gregory A. Huber, "Partisan Bias in Factual Beliefs about Politics," National Bureau of Economic Research Working Paper No. 19080, 4, accessed July 7, 2014, http://huber.research.yale.edu/materials/39_paper.pdf.

postmodernists, but they have brought it forcefully to our attention. In theory everyone's knowledge is biased, skewed, relative, although in practice many contemporaries proceed as if this insight applied to all views except their own.[14]

While this study of the factors influencing our understanding could lead to a sort of skepticism or relativism, I maintain that, while this conditioning influence cannot be eliminated, it can at least be reduced. Several exercises may contribute to that. One is interacting with those who differ from us, and especially those from different cultures and even different time periods. A second is writing one's own intellectual autobiography, inquiring as to what has influenced our way of thinking and what that effect has been.[15]

This should enable us to make certain adjustments or compensations to our understanding. It means recognizing that, because of our own built-in limitations and biases, we are probably not seeing matters accurately. Like a hunter who leads a moving target or a spear fisherman who drives the spear into the water at a point several inches from where the fish appears to be, to the extent we understand ourselves we can approach more closely to understanding correctly.

2. Cultivate conceptual empathy. By this I mean the ability to think one's way into the other's view and see things from his/her perspective. What frequently is actually done is that the other's understanding is interpreted through our own categories, which may be different, resulting in distortion. The process here is like learning another language rather than a translation or living within another culture rather than judging it from the perspective of our own.

On the first day of each course, I emphasize to my students that the first step in reviewing a book is "read the book!" and an essential subpoint is "including the preface," for that is frequently where the author lays out his/her intention in writing the book. I have read more reviews than I care to count in which the criticism is something like, "The author should have written the book the way I would have written it," or even, "The author's view is different from mine." Frequently the reader finds a contradiction within the author's writing that is actually a contradiction between the author's conceptions and

---

[14] Jacques Derrida states overtly that deconstruction cannot itself be deconstructed. "Force of Law: The Mystical Foundation of Authority," in *Deconstruction and the Possibility of Justice*, ed. Drucilla Cornell, Michel Rosenfeld, and David Gray Carlson (New York: Routledge, 1992), 14–15.

[15] For a fuller development of these suggestions, see my *Truth or Consequences*, 241–42.

those of the reader. The reader has strained the other's ideas through his own categories, distorting the former in the process. The criticism is therefore actually, "I disagree," and as I constantly remind my students, that is not a valid criticism. I have written on more than one paper, "So you and X disagree. Who's right, and what is your basis for saying that?"

Often the result is that we find from within the other's system of thought or worldview things make sense that from outside seem incoherent or irrational. I recall a missiologist once saying, "Unless you so immerse yourself within Islam that you are tempted to become a Muslim, you will never be able to influence Muslims." To a humanist, humanism makes good sense. To a Catholic, Catholicism makes good sense. The aim is to attempt to understand the other person and his/her beliefs and practices, not simply to pretend to do so. The dialogue will include interspersed genuinely sincere comments to the effect that "I understand why you would say that" or "I see what you mean." Training in debate helps develop this empathy, for the debater must be prepared to defend either the affirmative or the negative of the proposition under consideration.

3. Practice genuinely listening to the other person. Good listening is, unfortunately, a rather rare ability. In our day, with the wide use of social media, there appears to be a great deal of communication, but one wonders to what extent the free expression that takes place is matched by an equal amount of real attention being given. Social scientists are studying the qualities involved in listening. Some professionals study listening in order to become better able to communicate with clients. These two groups largely constitute the membership of the International Listening Association. Even at its convention, however, it was found that in the general population there is not a growing interest in listening, and most people believe listening does not require the development of any special skills.[16] Yet one of the keys to being listened to is to demonstrate real interest in what the other person is saying. Social science research has to some extent identified the qualities involved in effective listening.[17]

4. Emphasize precision of thought and expression. Much difficulty comes from ambiguity of understanding. In communication this means that one

---

[16] "Listen Up! Here's One Convention Where Talk Is Cheap," *The Wall Street Journal*, July 4, 2013, A1.

[17] E.g., Graham D. Bodie, "Listening as Positive Communication," *The Positive Side of Interpersonal Communication*, ed. Thomas J. Socha and Margaret J. Pitts (New York: Peter Lang, 2012), 109–26.

person in a dialogue understands something different from what the speaker intended. Thus either there appears to be agreement where there is not, or there appears to be disagreement when there is not, either of which situations leads to confusion and/or friction.

Part of the problem can be traced back to ourselves. Fuzzy thinking can easily be present when dealing with complex and abstract issues. This can be reduced, however, by the expansion and refinement of our conceptual store. That, in turn, is advanced by development of our vocabulary. Fine gradations of terminology advance the precision of our thinking. One book reviewer accused the author of sarcasm. It was apparent that the reviewer could not distinguish between sarcasm, satire, and irony.

Precision of thought and expression is an area that needs special attention in our day. Its lack is evident by the impulse to conflate several adjectives into one general adjective. There was a time when God was discussed in terms of his various attributes: power, knowledge, love, mercy, patience, etc. Much popular religious piety now seems to have reduced these to one: God is awesome![18]

5. *Be forthright in one's statements.* Respect for the other requires that we say what we mean and in as clear and unambiguous fashion as possible. Or, as one evangelical theologian put it, that we "lay all our cards on the table." A more general term for this is sincerity. In a postmodern age the tendency is toward obfuscation in expression. This may be simply an outgrowth of a particular view of the nature of truth. At times one suspects, however, that ambiguity is intentional so that, when accused of believing A, the person can say, "But I stated that I believe not-A." One professor was being examined for tenure at a Christian institution. The president and dean were inclined to grant this since he had stated that he believed a particular position on a doctrine in the school's doctrinal statement. When a sophisticated board member asked, however, whether he held a particular interpretation of that doctrine or a contradictory interpretation, the postmodern professor replied that he held both! The dean's jaw dropped, and the professor was denied tenure.

6. *Hold the other responsible.* While being diligent with our own thought and speech, there will be times when it is necessary to point out errors and

---

[18] Earlier theologies discussed the attribute of God's simplicity, which implied that all of his attributes were one and inseparable. While that term has largely dropped out of recent theological discussion, it now seems to have returned on the popular level in terms of his one attribute of awesomeness.

incivilities in the speech and conduct of another. Part of loving another means calling his/her attention to these shortcomings.

7. *Be diplomatic in one's statements.* Although this may seem inconsistent with the previous point, it is not. While we need to state our own views clearly and also point out erroneous views held by the other, there are more helpful and less helpful ways of doing this. Likening one's dialogue partners to the Taliban or mullahs does not tend to advance the discussion. One of the more helpful ways of seeking to correct the other is what I call "sneaking up on someone with the truth," approaching the issue indirectly and enabling the person to discover the truth rather than accusing him directly. A prime example of this was Nathan's confrontation of David (2 Sam 12:1–14). If he had asked, "What do you think of a king who has numerous wives and concubines but commits adultery with another man's wife?" the discussion would probably not have proven fruitful. Instead he told a parable of a man who had many sheep and took the neighbor's one little lamb, and David pronounced judgment on himself, not realizing that he had done so until Nathan said, "You are the man!" Jesus used similar rhetorical practices, such as in the parable of the good Samaritan (Luke 10:25–37, esp. v. 36).

8. *Pursue self-detachment.* One of the problems that sometimes contributes to incivility is taking discussions of ideas personally. We may come to attach our personal security to the success of our ideas, with a consequent elevation of emotion. Emotion, of course, is important in these dialogues, but it must be the right kind of emotion and at the right time and for the right reason. Defensiveness is not helpful in promoting civility.

It is helpful here to look to both Jesus' conduct and his teachings. As confrontational as Jesus sometimes was in his interaction with his opponents, particularly the Pharisees, he was not concerned to defend himself personally. Although he sought to establish his special relationship with the Father and to claim the spiritual prerogatives that were his, he did not respond to attacks on his person. His conduct in connection with his arrest, trial, and crucifixion is especially instructive.

Jesus also called his disciples to "deny themselves" and follow him (Matt 16:24; Mark 8:34; Luke 9:23). We have sometimes treated this admonition as if it meant to withhold from ourselves certain things, certain satisfactions. When examined more closely, however, a different insight emerges. The word Jesus used here is the same word used to describe Peter's threefold denial of

Jesus. What Peter did there was to say, "I don't know him."[19] When we hear something negative said about someone we do not know, we ordinarily do not take offense, nor do we swell with pride when we hear praise given to someone who is a total stranger to us. It is this sort of self-detachment that will enable objective response. It also is expressed in John the Baptist's words, "He must increase, but I must decrease" (John 3:30). Can we develop the powerful commitment to honor Christ and advance His cause in such a way that will enable us to deflect negative comments? If so, we will be spared the idea that we are being persecuted or hated, feelings which might lead us to respond uncivilly.

9. Act and speak with humility. When we are dogmatically sure we are right, we find more difficulty in respecting the views of others. We have spoken earlier of the conditioning factors upon our understanding. Theological factors are also involved. One of these is the sheer limitation upon our understanding, occasioned by the fact that we are human and finite, and God is infinite. An example of this teaching is found in Isaiah 55:8–9, "'For My thoughts are not your thoughts, and your ways My ways.' This is the LORD's declaration. 'For as heaven is higher than earth, so My ways are higher than your ways, and My thoughts than your thoughts.'" In addition to this natural difference between God and us, there is also a spiritual effect caused by human sin. Paul says, "In their case, the god of this age has blinded the minds of the unbelievers so they cannot see the light of the gospel of the glory of Christ, who is the image of God" (2 Cor 4:4). Although the Holy Spirit's work of regeneration and illumination serves to counter this blinding effect of sin (v. 6), some lingering influence remains. So the upshot of these two factors is that our understanding is imperfect and incomplete: "For now we see indistinctly, as in a mirror, but then face to face. Now I know in part, but then I will know fully, as I am fully known" (1 Cor 13:12).

What is needed here is to take seriously Oliver Cromwell's injunction: "I beseech in the bowels of Christ think it possible you may be mistaken."[20] Because we are finite human persons and our understanding is limited, we would perhaps be well advised to acknowledge that some of the evidence may be on the side of the other person. That should create in us a greater openness to listen to the other person. Economist Milton Friedman said, "You cannot

---

[19] The word in Matt 16:24 and Mark 8:34 (*aparneomai*) is the same word, and the word in Matt 10:33 and Luke 9:23 (*arneomai*) is a variation of the word used in Matt 26:34, 35, 75; Mark 14:30, 31, 72; and Luke 22:34, 61.

[20] Oliver Cromwell in a letter to the general assembly of the Church of Scottland, 1650.

be sure that you are right, unless you know the arguments against your view better than your opponents do."[21]

10. Related to the humility principle above is a corollary, namely, the willingness to agree partially. In the present political environment, some require absolute agreement on all points to work together with others. In the case of politics, Governor Chris Christie of New Jersey said, "If you're looking for someone who agrees with you 100 percent of the time, look in the mirror, because that's the only place you'll find someone like that." Actually, that was a bit of an overstatement, because many of us find we are sometimes of two minds on a given issue.

There is in politics currently something of a purity mentality. By that I mean the tendency to support only those who agree with one on every point. In the case of the far right, they succeeded in nominating conservative candidates against established candidates of their own party, who were conservative but not quite as conservative. The result was the loss of several key Senate races that probably could otherwise have been won, resulting in the election of candidates of the opposite party, who disagreed with them almost totally, and the passage of legislation they strongly opposed. They had forgotten, or at least failed to heed, Ronald Reagan's statement, "I would rather settle for 80 percent of the loaf than to lose the whole thing." Although this tends to be more on display with the far right, some on the far left politically also conduct themselves similarly.

I sometimes see similar behavior displayed by Christians. Agreement must be complete, or there can be no cooperation or, in some cases, even conversation. The problem is that it is easier to convince someone of a small matter than a large matter, or a part of an issue rather than the whole. A baseball manager whose team is behind by six runs sometimes has to remind his players that there is no such thing as a six- or seven-run home run. Change often has to be made incrementally.

11. Assume the best of one's dialogue partner. Part of the problem of incivility comes when we impute motives to the one with whom we are engaged. For example, if someone asserts something we believe or even know to be incorrect, we have a variety of options as to how to understand this phenomenon. As we suggested earlier, we need to consider the possibility that we are mistaken. Further, we may have misunderstood or misinterpreted the other

---

[21] Mary Ruth Yoe, "Market Force," *University of Chicago Magazine* 99, no. 3 (January–February 2007): 30.

person's statements, perhaps filtering them through our own categories, as we also mentioned earlier. If we have eliminated these possibilities, then we face additional options: either the person is prevaricating, or he/she is mistaken. A lie is a conscious misrepresentation of the facts. A mistake or error is an unintentional misrepresentation.

In general, then, if faced with this dilemma, our preferred choice or the default option should be to assume that the person is in error, or has overlooked some important consideration bearing upon this issue, rather than suggesting that this is a lie or other deliberate misdeed. While it may not be complimentary to question a person's knowledge (particularly if this is a scholar), it is less likely to lead to a breakdown of communication than questioning a person's character. Often in discourse conclusions are drawn on the basis of partial evidence. The omission of contrary evidence may be a case of lack of awareness or of deliberate attempt to misrepresent. For purposes of civility, it would be better to interpret these omissions as due to lack of awareness of these sources than to suggest they resulted from deliberate intention to misrepresent.

CONCLUSION

I have sometimes suggested a pledge one might take in the interest of civility. While we cannot be responsible for the other's part in the discussion, we can assume responsibility for our part, and might want to adopt something such as the following:

1. I will not point out the presuppositions of another's position without acknowledging that I have presuppositions myself.
2. I will not contend that another's view is historically conditioned without conceding that mine is also.
3. I will be more concerned not to misunderstand or misrepresent others' views than to claim that mine has been misunderstood or misrepresented.
4. I will be more concerned that my language be fair and objective than I am that others' language about me may not be.
5. I will not caricature my opponent's view to make my own appear more moderate.
6. I will not employ *ad hominem* arguments.
7. I will abstain from the use of pejorative language.
8. I will not impute motives or emotions to others.

9. I will think of intellectual arguments in terms of differences over ideas, not as personal disputes.

While those who differ with us are not our enemies and perhaps not even our opponents, Jesus' injunction to love our enemies (Matt 5:44) and to love our neighbor as ourselves (Matt 19:19) should contribute to the civility we seek to embody.

Convictional Clarity

R. Albert Mohler Jr.

T he Christian church was established as a community of conviction, and the church survives only as a movement marked by convictional clarity. As Western cultures become more and more secularized, Christians are required to clarify our convictions in the midst of an increasingly radical pluralism and a pervasive relativism on questions of truth.

In one sense the church now finds itself where it began. The apostles faced the inescapable challenge of clarifying Christian conviction as the early church began its witness and mission. In a real sense the New Testament reveals the efforts of the early church to define what we would now call a Christian worldview. Biblical Christianity rightly looks to the Bible, and the Bible alone, as the God-inspired source of revealed knowledge. Christianity is, and always has been, a religion of revealed truth. The teaching and preaching of that truth have been the responsibility of the church throughout the ages.

Now, once again, the great responsibility of the church is to be a people of convictional clarity. This is the task that drives all genuine Christian education, all true theology, and all faithful discipleship.

The Great Commission stands at the center of Christianity as the command of the risen Lord Jesus Christ for his church to proclaim the name of God in the world for the sake of all nations and God's glory among them. The church fulfills the commission by making disciples of Christ, teaching them to observe all that Christ has commanded his church to believe and obey (Matt 28:18–20). Christian discipleship that spreads the fame of God's name, then, is Christian truth-telling—telling the truth about the character of God by talking about what he has done in Christ for ultimate human flourishing across all cultures in every nation to the end of the age.

This conviction for Christian truth-telling has been the responsibility of the church since the first century. But we readily recognize that the context of Christian truth-telling—and for all truth-telling—has dramatically changed. The *truth* has not changed, but the *conditions* in which it is received will never be the same, either as they were in the first century or even as they were just fifteen years ago. The cultural context does not dictate the convictions of Christian truth-telling, but changing intellectual conditions do necessitate convictional clarity. Christian truth-telling, by definition, requires that the church work hard to be clear about its convictions and the truth claims the church bears into the world, into all cultures in every nation.

RETROSPECTIVE: CHANGING INTELLECTUAL CONDITIONS

Intellectual change takes place at different paces. Rarely has any model for intellectual change taken place with the velocity that is currently being experienced in Western societies and in the rest of the world as it is influenced by the West. This change is taking place before watching eyes and thinking minds to an extent and with a significance that is largely misunderstood and underestimated.

Some prophetic voices have recognized the scale and scope of the intellectual changes taking place in the West. Just over thirty years ago, Francis Schaeffer wrote of a shift in worldview away from one that was at least vaguely Christian in people's memory (even if they were not individually Christian) toward a completely different way of looking at the world. This new worldview was based on the idea that final reality is impersonal matter or energy shaped into its present form by impersonal chance. Significantly, Schaeffer observed that Christians in his time did not see this new worldview as taking the place of the Christian worldview that had previously dominated northern European and American cultures either by personal conviction or cultural impression. These two worldviews, one generally Christian and the other barely deistic, however, stood in complete antithesis to each other in content and also in natural results. These contrary ways of seeing the world would lead to disparate sociological and governmental results, specifically including the conception and implementation of law.

In 1983, writing just a few years after Francis Schaeffer wrote of a world-view shift, Carl F. H. Henry described the situation and future possibilities in terms of a strict dichotomy:

> If modern culture is to escape the oblivion that has engulfed the ear-lier civilizations of man, the recovery of the will of the self-revealed God in the realm of justice and law is crucially imperative. Return to pagan misconceptions of divinized rulers, or a divinized cosmos, or a quasi-Christian conception of natural law or natural justice will bring inevitable disillusionment. Not all pleas for transcendent au-thority will truly serve God or man. By aggrandizing law and human rights and welfare to their sovereignty, all manner of earthly leaders eagerly preempt the role of the divine and obscure the living God of Scriptural revelation. The alternatives are clear: we return to the God of the Bible or we perish in the pit of lawlessness.[1]

Writing even earlier, Henry had already identified the single greatest intel-lectual obstacle to a return to the God of the Bible. Released in 1976, Henry's first volume of his six-volume magnum opus, *God, Revelation, and Authority*, began with this first line: "No fact of contemporary Western life is more ev-ident than the growing distrust of final truth and its implacable questioning of any sure word."[2] This obstacle to the return to the authority of a Christian worldview is really part of a vicious circle that begins with the departure from at least a cultural impression of God's revealed authority: leaving a Christian worldview leads to a distrust of final truth and a rejection of universal author-ity, which then blockade the way back to the God of the Bible.

Secularization

American culture has secularized almost beyond its own memory of reli-gious authority. Every culture, civilization, or society operates under its own set of intellectual conditions that are prevalent at any given time. Honesty increasingly demands the description of American intellectual conditions as secular. *Secular*, in terms of contemporary sociological and intellectual con-versation, refers to the absence of any binding theistic authority or belief. It is both an ideology and a result. Secularization is not an ideology; it is a con-cept and a sociological process whereby societies become less theistic as they

---

[1] Carl F. H. Henry, *God, Revelation, and Authority*, vol. 6, *God Who Stands and Says Part 2* (Wheaton, IL: Crossway, 1999), 454.

[2] Carl F. H. Henry, *God, Revelation, and Authority*, vol. 1, *God Who Speaks and Shows, Preliminary Considerations* (Wheaton, IL: Crossway, 1999), 1.

become more modern. As societies move into conditions of deeper and more progressive modernity, they move out of situations in which there is a binding force of religious belief, and theistic belief in particular. These societies move into conditions in which there is less and less theistic belief and authority until there is hardly even a memory that such a binding authority had ever existed.

Modern secularization theory has unexpectedly failed and succeeded. The basic idea of secularization likely goes back to the Enlightenment, and it certainly goes back to the nineteenth and early twentieth centuries with Emil Durkheim and others. But only in the period during and after World War II was the social laboratory of Western societies open to the kind of consideration Peter Berger and other proponents of modern secularization began to give to the question of religion's place in a culture. Peter Berger joined with other sociologists to argue that modernity was producing a worldview with tremendous confidence in reason and rationality that would eventually crowd out and make unnecessary religious belief—certainly any binding religious belief. Books were written; encyclopedias were accumulated; theories were piled upon theories, all to explain how and why secularization would occur. Secularization was inexorable and inescapable. The only questions regarded how, why, and how long.

The secularization schedule of Europe covered about 150 years, accelerated at certain points by such events as the French Revolution and two world wars. As Peter Berger has admitted/boasted, secularization in America has failed, except where it has succeeded perfectly—American colleges and universities. For many reasons America did not track Europe's secularization. America has been the exception to secularization for decades. Whereas in some Scandinavian countries less than 2 percent of the people attend church regularly, an estimated 40 percent of Americans claim to be regular church attenders. And the vast majority of Americans at least say they believe in God. Those statistics have made American Christians believe that the majority of Americans share the same general beliefs about God.

But over the last fifteen years, that thought turns out to be erroneous. Secularization in America has not followed Europe except in American higher education. That modernity means the evaporation of religious belief, and binding authority has proved true in the American university culture. The closer one gets to an American college or university, the closer one gets to a secular public space—an intellectually secular place. As Peter Berger reminds us, those who are watching must understand that the engines of the culture are the cultural creative, the intellectual elites. And where are they gathered in the most concentrated form for optimal influence on the young? The college and university campus. The secularization America has largely avoided has been alive in its institutions of higher learning and has finally been unleashed on the nation through the many students who have had their worldview shaped by the few secular intellectual elites. Thus the intellectual conditions of America are quantitatively and qualitatively different from those that prevailed in the culture just fifteen years ago.

Theological liberalism has responded to American secularization with a campaign of accommodation. Secularization, in fact, provided the necessary conditions for theological liberalism; it could only emerge under the intellectual conditions of modernity. Secularization brought the hermeneutic of suspicion, the privileging of human reason over revelation, and the theme of liberation from intellectual authorities (especially the binding authority of theistic faith from a revealed book). These intellectual conditions created the context for theological liberalism to flourish. Before theological liberalism heresy was the only response to the prevailing intellectual conditions.

Unlike premodern heresy late modern theological liberalism attempts to bring the Christian faith into compliance with changing intellectual conditions. In the premodern age the intellectual conditions of orthodoxy defined and defied heresy. Theological liberalism, however, has an agenda of accommodation to changing intellectual conditions. Theological liberalism includes heresy but goes far beyond it, shifting from a supernatural to a naturalistic understanding of theology. Some, looking at churches and denominations, might opine that theological liberalism has failed: the associated institutions are collapsing. But secular historian David Hollinger points to the culture to argue that liberal Protestantism in particular won by losing—they won in the culture; they just lost their churches in the meantime.

Hollinger observes that theological liberalism has come to terms with and continued the momentum of American secularization by way of two intellectual moves. The first move was "cognitive demystification," the cognitive renegotiation of the faith that removes (demystifies) any necessary religious or theological explanation for the topic of conversation.[3] For example, Protestant liberals of the nineteenth century shifted from talking about the Christ of faith to merely the Jesus of history. Rather than a divinely revealed

---

[3] David A. Hollinger, *After Cloven Tongues of Fire: Protestant Liberalism in Modern American History* (Princeton, NJ: Princeton University Press, 2013), 6.

book, a deposit of divine revelation, Holy Scripture became an exemplary demonstration and representation of ancient Near Eastern literature. The faith, from beginning to end in every point of doctrinal concern, underwent the transformation of secularization. As the second move Hollinger describes how Protestant liberals took advantage of "demographic diversification."[4] As American culture became more pluralistic and people began to live and work alongside others who had different theological beliefs, two things happened: they began to pull in their convictions to avoid conflict, and they began to doubt the objective truth of their own truth claims. Regarding American evangelicals in particular, James Davison Hunter at the University of Virginia calls this phenomenon a process of "cognitive bargaining."[5]

On the other hand, some "posttheists" now think religion might be useful. Some of the intellectual elites of Europe are debating the ideological atheists, urging the cultural good of losing God but keeping religion. In his book *Religion Without God*, Ronald Dworkin makes the argument: We don't have to have God to have religion. Human beings turn out to be religious. What we need is a religion without God.[6]

Impossibility of Belief

American culture has secularized beyond the authority of the God of the Bible, and both the accommodation of theological liberalism and the denudation of posttheism will fail to recover that authority precisely because they cannot acknowledge that God. The problem of authority is a problem of belief. In his book *The Secular Age*, Canadian philosopher Charles Taylor confirms this problem of belief in Western civilization in terms of three sets of intellectual conditions. Every society and every individual operates under certain intellectual conditions, self-consciously or not. On the question of God, Taylor traces three Western intellectual epochs: pre-Enlightenment impossibility of unbelief; post-Enlightenment possibility of unbelief; late modern impossibility of belief.[7]

After the Enlightenment, Western intellectual conditions changed to make it possible for one not to believe in God. For most of human experience

---

[4] Ibid.

[5] See James Davison Hunter, *American Evangelicalism: Conservative Religion and the Quandary of Modernity* (New Brunswick, NJ: Rutgers University Press, 1983).

[6] Ronald Dworkin, *Religion Without God* (Cambridge, MA: Harvard University Press, 2013).

[7] See Charles Taylor, *The Secular Age* (Cambridge, MA: Harvard University Press, 2007).

in Western civilization, it has been impossible not to believe in God. That does not mean everyone was individually Christian (in Schaeffer's terms) or everyone had experienced conversion and was a regenerate believer. And it does not mean there were no skeptics or heretics. Before the Enlightenment, however, one could not explain the world without the Bible and its story. There was no alternative account of how the world came to be. No naturalistic worldview was available to people who lived in Western civilization throughout most of its centuries. Until Darwin presented an alternative to Genesis, the Christian worldview prevailed without a serious rival. It was impossible not to believe: it was impossible to explain life, from order in the universe to justice between two individuals, without explicit reference to revealed truth.

But that changed with the Enlightenment and the availability of alternative worldviews by which one could frame a comprehensive account of the world set over against the Christian worldview. Any worldview must answer at least four central questions: Why is there something rather than nothing? What has happened and is broken in the world? Is there any hope, and, if so, what is it? Where is history headed? With the Enlightenment came answers to these questions from a non-Christian framework (scientific naturalism, materialism, Marxism, etc.).

The intellectual conditions of Western culture have now become secularized so that it is impossible for those under such conditions to believe in God. As Charles Taylor observes, to be a candidate for tenure at a major American university is to inhabit a world in which it is virtually impossible to believe in God. Under the first set of Western intellectual conditions, not everyone was a Christian, but all were accountable to a Christian worldview because there was no alternative. Secularization in American culture has reversed the conditions: not everyone is a non-Christian, but all must operate under a secular worldview that denies the legitimacy of a Christian worldview. In 300 years, Western intellectual conditions have moved from an impossibility of unbelief to an impossibility of belief.

Significantly, Charles Taylor pinpoints this unbelief as a lack of cognitive commitment to a self-existent, self-revealing God. Secularization is not about religion. Taylor urges that people in the current hypersecularized culture in America often consider themselves to be religious or spiritual. Secularization, according to Taylor, is about belief in a personal God, one who holds and exerts authority. He describes the secular age as deeply "cross-pressured" in its personal experience of religion and rejection of the personal authority of God.[8] The issue is binding authority.

Outlaws and Authority

Christians are the intellectual outlaws under the current secular conditions. Entering a discussion on the basis of a theistic or theological claim is to break a cardinal rule of late modernity by moving from a proposition or question to a certain kind of *ought*. Some *oughts* remain, but the deontological language of command and law and authority has been explicitly secularized and carefully reduced in scope. Secularization in America has been attended by a moral revolution without precedent and without endgame. The cultural engines of progress driving toward personal autonomy and fulfillment will not stop until the human being is completely self-defining. This progress requires the explicit rejection of Christian morality for the project of human liberation. Christian minsters, theologians, and thinkers who stand on biblical authority break the rules by engaging the culture based on the self-revelation of a self-existent God of moral authority who has addressed his creatures with *oughts* and who does and will finally judge according to his laws and commands. By the fact that Christians enter every conversation as believers in the Lord Jesus Christ who are bound by biblical revelation means they cannot begin without breaking the rules. And those who break the rules are not welcome by those who make the rules.

As intellectual outlaws Christians must tell the truth to the secularized under the moral authority of the God of the Bible. Christians need to say with humility that we controlled the rules of public engagement for a long time without recognizing that was precisely what the church was doing. For centuries the church in America had the power and influence to control the rules until it lost that control during the process of accelerated secularization. Christians also must realize that regaining that kind of influence is a dim prospect because the new set of intellectual conditions makes the old rules not only unthinkable but intolerable. The secular mind makes liberation from the church's influence the necessary project for human flourishing.

In her book *How the West Really Lost God*, Mary Eberstadt summarizes: "For it is surely the case that in large stretches of the advanced West today many sophisticated people do not believe that the churches have any

---

[8] See Taylor, *The Secular Age*.

authority whatsoever to dictate constraints on individual freedom."[9] But the church cannot abdicate its responsibility for Christian truth-telling in a secular age. The secular intellectual conditions make it more challenging and difficult, seemingly impossible at times. Yet explicitly Christian truth-telling is the church's *raison d'etre*: "But you are a chosen race, a royal priesthood, a holy nation, a people for His own possession, so that you may proclaim the praises of the One who called you out of darkness into His marvelous light" (1 Pet 2:9). The God of the Bible has sent his church to tell the truth about the God of the Bible—about his laws and commands and about his grace and love.

PERSPECTIVE: THE CHURCH'S AUGUSTINIAN MOMENT

The church has arrived at its late modern Augustinian moment. When confronted by the convictions of a Christian worldview, the intellectual conditions of Augustine's day gave rise to his great work, *The City of God*. In his own lifetime and in that work, the moment came for Saint Augustine to think and speak in terms of distinct but overlapping kingdoms: the kingdom of God and the kingdom of man. Augustine told the truth as he heard it from the apostle Paul, who has revealed from God that Christians are citizens of the kingdom of heaven who also live as citizens of earthly kingdoms until the end of this age. This does not require the adoption of a strict "two kingdom theology," as in the Lutheran tradition. But thinking with Paul does mean leaning into Augustine's insights to understand God's design of two kingdoms for this age and the church's place and responsibility in that design.

The kingdom of God is permeated by the love of God in order to penetrate the kingdom of man. As Augustine rightly observed, the two kingdoms of God and man are animated respectively by the two different loves of God and man. More specifically the animating power of the love of God is found in the gospel; apart from the gospel man remains trapped in the love of man and condemned for no love of God. But in the drama of this dilemma, God reveals his design for the church: the church bears the love of God in the truth of the gospel from the kingdom of God into the kingdom of man. That "God loved the world in this way: He gave His One and Only Son, so that everyone who believes in Him will not perish but have eternal life" is a truth *for the world* (John 3:16). The church is created and sustained by the gospel so the church proclaims the gospel in the world and for the world, regardless

---

[9] Mary Eberstadt, *How the West Really Lost God: A New Theory of Secularization* (West Conshohocken, PA: Templeton Press, 2013), 38.

of the world's intellectual conditions for truth. Love of God and love of neighbor, the first and second commandments, must come together in a late modern Augustinian moment to remind the church that if we are faithful to the Scriptures we must be faithful to truth-telling, whatever the conditions, whatever the character of the age. Christians can no longer delude themselves into thinking Christian truth can be negotiated down such that the church can remain silent in service to the gospel. The church is a "chosen race" not to enjoy the love of God apart from the world but to take the love of God into the world by proclaiming the truth of the gospel across all cultures in every nation unto the end of the age.

The gospel is at stake in man's knowledge of himself as a sinner. To confuse the sinner about his own sinfulness is to suggest he has less need of Christ. Leaving sin hidden in intellectual conditions that deny the existence and moral authority of God makes the gospel unintelligible. The late modern project demands that Christians either remain silent or join the intellectual conditions by, for example, redefining human sexuality to normalize what the Scriptures clearly condemn. But both silence and accommodation to secularization deny the authority of Scripture and lie to the world about its wretched condition and the beauty of human flourishing in the gospel.

So, how "in the world" do Christians tell the truth?

Arguments based on natural law are working against Christian truth-telling. If the mode of Protestant liberalism is certainly wrong, if accommodationism is not the proper agenda, then is there some form of neutral ground? Is there a neutral alternative? Can Christians accomplish gospel ends through Christian truth-telling without recourse to explicit Christian language and biblical authority? Some propose a shift from scriptural argumentation to persuasion by means of natural law. But the moral impulses of the secular mind follow a form of natural law: people under secular intellectual conditions look at the *is* as they currently see it and immediately assume it is an *ought*.

Sexual liberationists, for instance, argue: "People are born this way. This is who I am. This is nature." Christians, of course, believe in natural law. We believe that by common grace and common revelation the truths that reflect human flourishing are revealed in the fabric of the world. The problem with natural-law arguments, however, is that the secular mind does not understand it is looking at *fallen* nature. On the other side of Genesis 3 is a residual revelation that is true to God and his character found in his creation, but that nature is distorted by the comprehensive effects of sin on both man and nature itself. So those who argue for sexual liberation do so on the basis of their own natural law argument, based on nature as it appears to them. They misread nature not in terms of how it appears to them but in terms of its reality as revealed by its Creator. All creation is crying out human sinfulness and falleness and curse from which redemption must come.

To penetrate the world with the love of God, the church must rely on the word of God and the gospel of Christ. There is no neutral ground for the gospel; there is no secular plausibility for the binding moral authority of God. Christians should be keen students of the natural law but students who are first evangelical theologians who know how nature must be read and understood. Natural-law arguments can bring fullness and illustration and comprehensiveness to the Christian worldview from what is already known from Scripture. Neither the natural law nor any other alternative, however, can serve as a substitute for Scripture in any sense. But such a situation does not hinder Christian truth-telling; it heightens the church's need to take seriously what its Lord has given it to do. The Lord has commissioned the church to be redemptive truth-tellers, and he has given it his word and his gospel for the task.

PROSPECTIVE: CONVICTIONAL CLARITY FOR CHRISTIAN TRUTH-TELLING

In its Augustinian moment the church finds itself in Matthew 10. Jesus exhorts his disciples: "What I tell you in the dark, speak in the light. What you hear in a whisper, proclaim on the housetops" (Matt 10:27). The evangelical church in this generation, and in any foreseeable generation to come, must recognize that we must learn new skills in Christian truth-telling. We must display a new attitude. If nothing else, we have to display the recognition that we are now understood to be the outlaws rather than the judges of conversations. We are those who come in breaking the rules rather than making the rules. We have to be invited into some conversations where otherwise we would have been the conveners. We must separate our Christian truth-telling from alien agendas. That's tough; and sometimes in terms of this cultural context, it's almost impossible. We all show up as fully orbed human beings with all of our allegiances and alliances and everything that comes with us. But in so far as it is possible, one of the skills we must learn is demonstrating a new attitude in terms of freeing ourselves from every alien agenda other than telling the truth. We must find our accountability within the church of the

Lord Jesus Christ and in no other place. But we have to say what we know. We have no choice but to speak what has been revealed, what leads to human flourishing—that word that saves.

In Matthew 10:26 Jesus says, "There is nothing covered that won't be uncovered and nothing hidden that won't be made known." And it is explicitly in the context of sending his disciples out into a hostile world in which truth-telling is going to be so difficult that he illustrates it with specific patterns of response in light of the rejection. "What I tell you in the dark, speak in the light. What you hear in a whisper, proclaim on the housetops" (Matt 10:27). Our temptation is going to be to lower our voice and be reticent to speak. Our temptation is going to be everything that is precisely wrong. Jesus did not say you are going to face opposition so lower your voice. The intellectual conditions of every society in a fallen world are always hostile to the proclamation of the gospel. Our times are uniquely hostile, but so were the times of these disciples. Counterintuitively, Jesus authoritatively says to the Twelve, "What I tell you in the dark, speak in the light." He speaks the same words to us through this unchanging, eternal word. Our responsibility is to know that what we receive in the dark we are to speak in the light.

The church must learn how to speak boldly in the light in ways that are skillful, prayerful, humble, and fully obedient. The church must confess that it is not our responsibility to determine the message but only to preach it, not to devise it but to take it, not to market it but to bear witness to it. May we learn the skills God would have us to learn in this age that we may do exactly what Jesus commissioned the apostles to do in the first century. The church must tell the truth in the light until "the kingdom of the world has become the kingdom of our Lord and of His Messiah, and He shall reign forever and ever" (Rev 11:15).

In other words, the church must learn anew the skill of convictional clarity and the passion of Great Commission urgency. These are not merely the fundamentals of the Christian worldview. They are the essence of Christian faithfulness in this and every generation.

What God Hath Joined Together

Proclamation and Witness as Twin Pillars in
the Ministry of the Apostle Paul

Acts 20:17–38

Robert Smith Jr.

T he apostle Paul's ministry addressed three significant questions for believers: first, the anthropological question: who am I? *Homo sapiens* are
human beings and not amoeba or protozoa, one-cell organisms that evolve
into human construction. Psalm 8:5 asserts that God made man a little lower
than angels and crowned man with honor. Second, the theological question:
where did I come from? Genesis 1:26 announces that man came from the
hand of God. God spoke everything in creation into existence. However,
when he got ready to bring humanity into existence, he got his hands dirty by
stooping down and making man out of the dust of the earth (Gen 2:7). Man
is made in the image of God—the *imago Dei* (Gen 1:26). Finally, the eschatological question: where am I going?

The gospel bears both good and bad news. It is good news for those who
believe its message and are saved and bad news for those who deny its message and are lost (Mark 16:15–16). Ecclesiastes 12:7 declares that "the dust
returns to the earth as it once was, and the spirit returns to God who gave it."
This essay will draw upon four knowledge areas Paul employed in serving his
Ephesian congregations. Like the apostle Paul faithful and effective ministers

should know four things about the persons they serve: their names, the nature of their problems, their necessary virtues, and their real needs.

Paul knew the names of his people. The apostle Paul called for a pastors' conference to be held at Miletus. He sent for the elders who served in Ephesus. Sending for them implied an RSVP for certain elders to attend the conference; therefore, names were attached to the invitation. Paul knew their names because he had spent time with them. Verse 18 states that Paul had invested time with these elders, and verse 31 tells us he had given three years of his life to pour into these servants. Paul knew these individuals. This is customary with Paul. In Romans 16:3–16 Paul sends a letter by Phoebe in which he lists the names of many persons who had served in the ministry with him. Paul was patterning himself after his Lord who called the names of the disciples who would be in training under him and would later carry on his work after his ascension (Mark 3:13). Even Adam named the animals that came to him, and whatever he named them that is what they were called (Gen 2:19).

Paul knew the nature of the problems of his people. Paul recognized the Ephesian church as susceptible to heresy. In verse 30, Paul tells the elders to watch out for persons within the flock who come to distort the truth in order to gather disciples for their own work. In verse 31, Paul reminds these elders that he has been warning them about this for three years. In Ephesians 4:14, Paul desires that the Christians in the Ephesian church be mature and no longer infants who are tossed and driven by waves and winds of false doctrine. This is certainly a significant concern for Jesus, who knew that false teachers would come as wolves dressed in sheep's clothing, distorting the truth and destroying the flock (Matt 7:15).

Paul knew the necessary virtues of his people. Verses 36–38 describe one of the most poignant and emotionally moving scenes in the Bible. In verse 25, Paul tells the elders they would not see him again. They loved him and responded by kneeling down and praying with him, then weeping, embracing, and kissing him. The virtues of expressive love and appreciation were evident. Both Paul and the elders needed to express their love and appreciation for each other. Paul knew an effective leader must be both cranial and cardiological in his service. Head and heart must be inextricably expressed. Paul understood that efficient leaders follow the dictates of Jesus who said, "Love the Lord your God with all your heart, with all your soul, and with all your mind" (Matt 22:37).

Paul knew the real needs of his people. The most important need of the people he served was the Word of God. In verse 20, Paul reminds these elders that he had not kept back anything that was profitable but had taught them publicly and from house to house. Paul balanced the public teaching of the word in Ephesus. He taught the Word of God publicly for two years in the school of Tyrannus (Acts 19:9–10). He also taught the Word of God in house churches and probably in the midst of individual families in their own homes. He summarized his perception of the Word of God being their most important real need by saying he had not hesitated to declare unto them the whole counsel of God (Acts 20:27).

THE APOSTLE PAUL AND THE WHOLE COUNSEL OF GOD

I define the "whole counsel of God" *as a concept that unites and ties together every passage of Scripture so that it relates to the overall plan and comprehensive purpose of God revealed in the Bible through the Holy Spirit* in order to magnify Jesus Christ. This definition is saturated in intratrinitarian presence. It relates the overall plan and comprehensive purpose of *God*. It is revealed in the Bible through the *Holy Spirit*, and its ultimate objective is to magnify *Jesus Christ*. Paul provides a paradigm for his similar proclamation in Acts 20:27. He calls it the whole counsel of God.

Paul had only an Old Testament Bible and would have reflected on several Christological emphases in the Old Testament. For example, Joseph went to look for his brothers by the order of his father, Jacob, and was informed by an anonymous man that his brothers went to Dothan (Gen 37:17). After Joseph arrived in Dothan, the brothers apprehended him and sold him to the Ishmaelites who transported him to Egypt where he would serve as the chamberlain in Potiphar's house. Potiphar's wife falsely accused him of molestation. He was imprisoned, remembered to Pharaoh by the butler, and had the opportunity to interpret Pharaoh's dream. He recommended that Pharaoh store grain in Egypt during the fruitful years of the harvest season so there would be grain in Egypt during the years of the foretold famine. Pharaoh complied with Joseph's recommendation and executed his plan. Thus Joseph saved not only the nation of Egypt from starvation but also his own brothers who had come to Egypt to buy grain. By saving his brothers, Judah would be spared. Because Judah was spared, the tribe that would lead to Jesus was salvaged, and Christ came into the world to save sinners. Therefore, Genesis

37:17 greatly factors into the whole counsel of God because it relates to *the overall plan and purpose of God.*

The book of Ruth relates to the overall plan and purpose of God also. It opens with the announcement that Naomi and her husband, Elimelech, lived during the days of the judges in which there was *no king.* This couple lived in the city of Bethlehem, the house of bread. During those days there was a great famine. Elimelech and Naomi found it necessary to leave Bethlehem because there was *no bread* in Bethlehem, the house of bread. They journeyed to the cursed country of Moab, and while there Elimelech died. Elimelech and Naomi's two sons, Mahlon and Chilion, also died. There was *no son.* Three great absences—*no king, no bread, no son*! Naomi received word that the famine had been lifted in Bethlehem, and she made her way back home because there was *now bread* in the house of bread. While there Naomi counseled Ruth regarding her relative Boaz. Boaz and Ruth would eventually marry, and *a son* would be born. The community called the boy the son of Naomi (Ruth 4:17). That son would eventually contribute to the kingly line of Jesus because the son of Boaz and Ruth, Obed, would become the father of Jesse. Jesse would become the father of David. Through David, Israel's greatest *king,* Jesus, the King of kings, would come—born in a stable in the city of Bethlehem where there would be *no room* in the inn. Hosea 11:1 announces, "Out of Egypt I called My son." Hosea, an eighth-century BC prophet, looks back at the Exodus in the fourteenth century BC and reminds Israel as a nation that God considered the nation a son. After 400 years of incarceration in Egypt, God delivered them. Matthew also uses the Hosea 11:1 text, stating that God called his Son out of Egypt. Matthew, writing in the first century AD, employs the Hosea 11:1 text, but he is not referring to the fourteenth century BC historical event of the Exodus. Rather, he is referring to the first century AD announcement made to Joseph by the angel Gabriel that Joseph can bring Mary and Jesus, the Son of God, back to Canaan. Herod the Great, who sought the life of Jesus, was dead. Thus Matthew 2:15 provides a *sensus plenior,* or fuller sense, of the interpretation of Hosea 11:1. This contributes to *the overall plan and comprehensive purpose of God.*

In Acts 2:22–24, according to the predetermined counsel of God, Jesus is arrested by the chief priests, scribes, and elders; is crucified; and is raised by God from the dead. These ecclesiastical leaders appear to be unilaterally executing Jesus according to their own whims and wishes. However, God had predetermined that Jesus would be crucified before the creation of the world; Jesus was the Lamb slain from the foundation of the world (Rev 13:8). Therefore, the crucifixion was not plan B as a reaction to the fall; the crucifixion was plan A as a preaction before the fall. God had anticipated the fall in eternity past. Acts 2:24 provides the hope following the crucifixion: God raised Jesus from the dead.

The whole counsel of God permeates time and is intratrinitarian in nature. God the Father provided the overall plan and comprehensive purpose. God the Son was elected to execute the plan through his own execution. However, the Father who elected the Son in the incarnation when the Word became flesh (John 1:14) rejected the Son in the crucifixion when Jesus cried, "My God, My God, why have You forsaken Me?" (Mark 15:34). However, God the Holy Spirit raised the Son on the third day in the resurrection according to plan A. The apostle Paul states that the same Spirit who raised Jesus from the dead will also quicken our mortal bodies (Rom 8:11). Though the triune God is mystery and can never be completely understood, he must always be worshipped in his intratrinarian nature. God the Holy Spirit reveals the whole counsel of God the Father portrayed through the Bible to capture *the overall plan and comprehensive purpose of God in order to magnify Jesus Christ.*

Even to consider discussing the concept of the whole counsel of God is an audacious enterprise. Trying to capture the whole counsel of God in teaching and preaching is like trying to capture the wind with a net! How does one talk about the whole counsel of God? Paul says in Romans 11:33–34: "Oh, the depth of the riches both of the wisdom and the knowledge of God! How unsearchable His judgments and untraceable His ways! For who has known the mind of the Lord? Or who has been His counselor?" Who can counsel the One who is known as "Wonderful Counselor" (Isa 9:6)? How does one even begin to ponder the concept of the whole counsel of God when the psalmist declares of God, "Your way went through the sea and Your path through the great waters, but Your footprints were unseen" (Ps 77:19)? How does one reflect on a God who is so mysterious that he chooses to move without leaving a footprint behind him for observation or study? How does the believer follow God the Holy Spirit who like the wind does not provide the whereabouts of his coming or his going (John 3:8)? This is the God that John Calvin posits—the *Deus absconditus* (hidden God) and the *Deus revelatus* (revealed God). This is the God of Rudolf Otto's *mysterium tremendum fascinosus* (the mysterious tremendous God who encounters his children and leaves them transfixed with tremors). This is the God that calls worshippers to adore him

while they tremble in his presence. How can one even meditate with comprehension on the whole counsel of God when God's ways are higher than our
ways and his thoughts are higher than our thoughts (Isa 55:8–9)? Yet this is
the task of Christian ministers, to always assume a point of departure in discussing the deep things of God with the realization that we will never arrive at
the place of total comprehension. This is the enormous challenge the apostle
Paul took up in his ministry of proclamation and witness.

THE APOSTLE PAUL'S MINISTRY OF
PROCLAMATION AND WITNESS

The apostle Paul was a doxological dancer. My definition of a doxological
dancer calls for one who communicates the doctrinal truths of Scripture with
accuracy and ardor so the exuberant hearer exults in the exaltation of God.[1]
The early church grew quickly. Approximately 3,000 persons were saved on
the day of Pentecost during the preaching of Peter and the apostles (Acts
2:41). The first thing Luke the historian mentions following their salvation
is that these converts continued steadfastly in the apostles' doctrine. What is
doctrine? The late, celebrated historian Jaroslav Pelikan once said, "What the
church of Jesus Christ believes, teaches and confesses on the basis of the Word
of God, this is Christian doctrine."[2] For Paul, doctrine is not to be endured;
rather it is to be enjoyed. It is not dull; rather it dances and is exciting. For
example, in Romans 1–11 Paul piles on prodigious mountains of doctrine
about hamartiology (sin), justification, sanctification, glorification, divine
sovereignty and election, anthropology (humanity), creation, pneumatology
(Holy Spirit), Christology, and the Trinity. Paul then closes chapter 11 with
verses 33–36 in which he sings his theology. Thus Paul doxologizes theology
and causes it to dance.

The apostle Paul was an exegetical escort. According to my definition an
exegetical escort is one who escorts the hearer by the Word of God into the
presence of Christ the Son of God through the power of the Spirit of God
for the purpose of transformation.[3] There must be intratrinitarian presence
within the ministry of those who serve the Lord's church. The apostle Paul
knew transformation will never come through our words or our work; it will

---

[1] See Robert Smith Jr., *Doctrine that Dances* (Nashville: B&H, 2008), 107.
[2] See Jaroslav Pelikan, *The Christian Tradition: A History of the Development of Doctrine*,
vol. 1 (Chicago: University of Chicago Press, 1971), 1.
[3] See Smith, *Doctrine that Dances*, 75.

only come through the Word of God. He was not called to transform; he was called to inform. His ministry was patterned after the greatest exegetical escort, Jesus. In Luke 24:13–36, Jesus, the Son of God, escorts two at-large disciples by the Word of God. He leads them from a slow heart (v. 25) to a burning heart (v. 32). They are transformed and experience transformation in three areas: First, they obtain *learning*; their eyes are opened, for he opened them to the Scriptures (Luke 24:32). Second, they experience *burning*; their hearts burned within them (Luke 24:32). Third, they acquire *yearning*; they immediately leave Emmaus and return to Jerusalem to tell the disciples that the Lord is risen indeed (Luke 24:33–35).

The apostle Paul not only preached and taught others, but he also experienced what he preached and taught. His ministry was one that gave evidence to a marriage of exegesis and experience. The ink of his preaching and teaching was turned into the blood of his *kerygma* (proclamation) and *didache* (teaching). The *was-ness* of the biblical story became the *is-ness* of his life, work, and ministry. His hearers heard their story in his story. The late, great Scottish preacher Arthur John Gossip eulogized his wife with a sermon entitled "When Life Tumbles In, What Then?" It was based on Jeremiah 12:5: "If you have raced with runners and they have worn you out, how can you compete with horses? If you stumble in peaceful land, what will you do in the thickets of the Jordan?" Gossip was dealing with the necessity of having faith during the crises of life. His theology was not a prosperity theology but rather an adversity theology. He related to his hearers at that funeral service that he had been to the bottom and found it was solid! Gossip also adamantly acknowledged that "people in the sunshine *may* believe the faith, but we in the shadow *must* believe it. We have nothing else."[4] The whole counsel of God, which investigates the mind and purpose of God, is worthy of our trust and is able to keep us in the slippery places of life. Those who listen to Christian leaders and observe them going through crises want to know if they really believe what they have been preaching and teaching. Like Paul's life, the leader's life must report a resounding "Yes!"

The Greek word *mega* means "big or large." It is used in a plethora of ways during our conversations: *megabyte, megadeal, megahertz, megacorporation, megabucks.* We even use *megachurch.* A megachurch is one that has a membership of 2,000 or more people. Many churches become mega because

---

[4] Arthur John Gossip, *The Hero in Thy Soul: Being an Attempt to Face Life Gallantly* (New York: Charles Scribner's Sons, 1929), 111.

of the attractiveness of their ministries. They are able to attract large numbers of people by diverse ministry offerings. However, many of these churches, though they have the power of attraction, do not have the power of retention—keeping power! God is interested in numbers. Acts 2:41 records that about 3,000 people were added to the church following Peter's pentecostal sermon. God is interested in numbers. Second Peter 3:9 says that "the Lord does not delay his promise, as some understand delay, but is patient with you, not wanting any to perish but all to come to repentance." God is interested in numbers. But a megachurch with meganumbers without a *megagospel* does not fulfill the desire of God. In order to draw persons to the church, we must have a megagospel. A megagospel will produce mega-Christians who are motivated to carry the whole gospel to the whole world. The megagospel not only attracts but also retains. Sermonic "happy meals" will not nourish believers. Homiletical gimmicks and novelties will not mature believers. *Socializing* the gospel will not edify believers. The minister must *gospelize* the social— that is, let the gospel speak to social inequities by ministering to the needy and following it up with a message that transforms the heart. In other words, every social ministry must serve as a platform to give the gospel an audience for the proclamation of its holistic message. No social ministry points to itself but rather exists to point to Christ who is the gospel. Feeding the poor is a prelude for offering the poor Jesus, the Bread of life. Ministering to the grief stricken is a precursor for introducing people to Christ, who binds up broken hearts and provides a purpose for living beyond grief. He is the One who turns *mourning* into *morning*. Every social ministry within the church exists to provide an opportunity for preaching the gospel.

At a recent national preaching conference, Dr. Ralph Douglas West, pastor of the Church Without Walls, Houston, Texas, which has more than 22,000 members, related that he was repeatedly asked by pastors how he grew such a megachurch. His response was simply, "I just preach the gospel." Several pastors continued to press him on this matter, inquiring about the methodology and philosophy he used to amass such a large following. His response was consistent and simple: "I just preach the gospel." The gospel does not need to be adjusted; it needs to be trusted. While the church ministers to the holism of humanity, it must be done by grounding the message in the biblical witness to Jesus Christ. Christian ministers need to preach and teach this gospel with the burning lips of Isaiah, the burning heart of Jeremiah, and the broken heart of Hosea. There must be an incarnational presence, the Word must become flesh. The apostle Paul's ministry of proclamation and witness reflected the employment, empowerment, and enjoyment of a megagospel that attracted sinners through justification, retained believers through sanctification, and prepared saints for glorification.

In proclaiming the whole counsel of God, the apostle Paul's ultimate purpose was to magnify Jesus Christ. Paul did not attempt to make Christ bigger; that is impossible. Rather, he sought to present Christ, *the incarnate Word of God*, through the Bible, *the written Word of God*, as he proclaimed the gospel through *the spoken Word of God* as the only means of spiritual transformation. Proclaiming the whole counsel of God is not merely a promulgation of a proposition; rather, for the apostle Paul, it is the proclamation of the person of Jesus Christ. Pilate stands before Jesus and asks a propositional question: "What is truth?" (John 18:38). It is astounding that the person of Truth is standing before Pilate. Pilate ignores the presence of the Truth, Jesus, in search of a propositional truth. Jesus said, "I am . . . the truth" (John 14:6). Similarly, Thomas the disciple asked for the direction or route to the place Jesus was going to prepare. He said, "We don't know where You're going. How can we know the way?" (John 14:5) He was seeking a route and ignoring the personification of the route. Jesus informed him about a person and not a direction: "I am the way" (John 14:6). Martha, the sister of Mary and Lazarus of Bethany, believed she would see her dead brother Lazarus again. She believed in the doctrine of the resurrection and said to Jesus, "I know that he will rise again in the resurrection at the last day" (John 11:24). Her eschatology was correct, but her Christology needed to be adjusted and extended. She failed to recognize that the person of the resurrection was speaking to her. Jesus said to Martha, "I am the resurrection and the life. The one who believes in Me, even if he dies, will live. Everyone who lives and believes in Me will never die—ever" (John 11:25–26). Those of us who would proclaim and teach the whole counsel of God to the whole world must always showcase and highlight the person of Jesus Christ along with the accompanying propositional truth about Jesus Christ.

We must recognize what the German theologian Helmut Thielicke understood—that the crib and the cross are the same wood. Too often we teach and preach Christmas and Easter as separate events as if they are not related. Christmas songs ought to be sung during Easter, and Easter songs ought to be sung during Christmas to remind congregants that Christmas and Easter are inextricably connected. Ultimately the crib and the cross must point toward the crown, which represents the victory and reign of God in Christ through the power of the Spirit who raised Jesus from the dead. Sermon and song that tie together the crib, the cross, and the crown must share sacred space in both singing and speaking theology.

The apostle Paul's ministry anticipated the great reformer Martin Luther's conviction concerning the concept of *ad fontes*, a return to the sources. He also anticipated Martin Luther in emphasizing in his preaching and witnessing ministry the five *solas* of the Reformation: *sola Christus*, by Christ alone (1 Tim 2:5); *sola fides*, by faith alone (Rom 5:1); *sola gratia*, by grace alone (Eph 2:8); *sola scriptura*, by Scripture alone (Matt 4:4); and *soli Deo gloria*, for the glory of God alone (1 Cor 10:31). And yet Paul presented these theological truths in fresh ways by using the contemporary images of a runner, a wrestler, an accountant, a soldier, a farmer, and many other images that connected with his audience.

The apostle Paul proclaimed and gave witness to the whole counsel of God for the whole world through the *power of the Holy Spirit*. The Holy Spirit of God reveals *the overall plan and comprehensive purpose of God the Father to the hearer for the purpose of magnifying Jesus Christ, the Son of God*. Across the breadth of his writings, Jonathan Edwards, the great Protestant theologian, was convicted that God has forever known Himself in a sweet and holy society as Father, Son, and Holy Spirit. Too often the Holy Spirit is the neglected or forgotten God in our proclamation and witness. Calvin believed preaching could not occur until there was an internal witness of the Spirit revealing the truths of the text and applying the implications of the preached Word of God to the hearer, thus bringing about conviction and transformation. It is the Spirit who reveals the meaning of the inscripturated Word, which is *God breathed* (2 Tim 3:16).

Several years ago I had the privilege of preaching for the Billy Graham School of Evangelism, which was held in a large hotel on Times Square in New York City. I wanted to walk up and down Times Square because I had seen its many sights and heard its many sounds on television, particularly on New Year's Eve. I became an obvious example of a tourist. After taking a few steps, I stood still and looked around. I took a few more steps and was caught up in the glamour and glitter of my surroundings. I spent a great amount of time as a *tourist* beholding the Times Square activity because of my high interest level. However, those who had seen it all many times were obviously *residents*. Their gait and cadence were fast. They did not look up or look around—they only looked forward, moving toward their destination. They had seen it all before.

The apostle Paul proclaimed the whole counsel of God as a *tourist* and not as a *resident*. He knew he could not see it all or know it all. The ministry of proclamation and witness never became boring to him, for he could not capture or comprehend the unfathomable depth of God. Ministers of the gospel must approach the God of the text and the text of God with a sense of second naiveté, as children who are experiencing the text for the first time and being encountered by God in a fresh way. They must examine the text with ecstasy and delve into it with delight. It must not be a mundane moment but rather a magnificent movement. The familiar must become unfamiliar. That which seemed to be simple must be rendered stupendous. The whole counsel of God must be viewed through the eyes of a *tourist* of the text and not as a *resident* of the Scripture. This is the DNA of the ministry of the apostle Paul. This is his theological genetic coding.

Paul was caught up and taken to the third heaven where he saw and heard things that he was not permitted to talk about when he preached and witnessed the profound truths of the gospel. God had pronounced a moratorium on his speech, for the experience Paul had in the third heaven could not be comprehended by those who heard him. His hearers were not celestially conditioned to understand what Paul had experienced. In spite of Paul's third-heaven rendezvous, he continued to approach the ministry of the Word like a child experiencing the text for the first time. Paul's practice in ministry was to crawl up into the cranium of Yahweh and remain there long enough to emerge with the pronouncement, "Oh, the depth of the riches both of the wisdom and the knowledge of God! How unsearchable His judgments and untraceable His ways! For who has known the mind of the Lord? Or who has been His counselor?" (Rom 11:33–34). Let us examine the ministry of the apostle Paul through the bifocal lens of proclamation and witness portrayed in Acts 20:17–38.

A SERMON ON THE WITNESS OF THE APOSTLE PAUL

Introduction

Following the reasoning of Peter's statement in Acts 4:20, "We are unable to stop speaking about what we have seen and heard," Paul's ministry must be mirrored by our twenty-first-century ministry in the execution of proclamation through our witness. *Proclamation does not exist for our own privatized enterprise, but rather for the promulgation of the gospel.* Whenever proclamation is an end in itself rather than a means to the end of accomplishing the Great Commission, proclamation has forgotten its primary role.

In Acts 20:17–38, the apostle Paul delivers his third speech. This speech is unique in that it is delivered to an entire Christian audience. The first speech was given to a Jewish audience in the Syrian city of Antioch of Pisidia (Acts 13:14). The second speech was proclaimed in the city of Athens, Greece, before a congregation of Athenian philosophers and pagans (Acts 17:16). In this third address Paul speaks to the Ephesian leaders at Miletus (Acts 20:17). Paul has sailed to Miletus. His desire is to speak to these religious leaders once again. It would take a few days for Paul's emissaries to travel from Miletus to Ephesus to invite the Ephesian leaders to a pastors' conference there. This question lingers: if Paul wanted to address the Ephesian leaders, why didn't he take a ship that would land in Ephesus? Perhaps Paul decided not to sail to Ephesus because it was too dangerous. In Acts 19:23–31, Demetrius the silversmith had stirred up a mob to threaten Paul's life because he was an economic liability to the industry that produced figurines of the idolatrous image of Artemis. Because of Paul's preaching, individuals who had been involved in black magic brought their magical-art books to the city square and burned them. Paul was not good for business and by the grace of God was able to escape Ephesus with his life. Therefore, he probably chose not to put himself in danger in that city again.

Additionally, Paul probably chose not to sail to Ephesus because he wanted to get to Jerusalem in time to celebrate Pentecost. He had already missed the celebration of Passover at Jerusalem. Furthermore, he had collected an offering from Gentile believers to deliver to the Jews in Jerusalem who were suffering. One can envision the boat from Ephesus landing at the port in Miletus. The persons who walked across the plank to greet Paul were elders, overseers, and pastors whom Paul undoubtedly knew. Perhaps some of them were former disciples of John the Baptist who in Acts 19:1–2 heard Paul ask them, "Did you receive the Holy Spirit when you believed?" These former disciples had only heard and believed the baptism or doctrine of John the Baptist (Acts 19:3–4). When Paul explained the whole counsel of God more fully and laid hands on them, they received the Holy Spirit (Acts 19:4–6). Perhaps some of these leaders were former workers in black magical arts who had been saved and now lived their lives by the power of the Holy Spirit. All likely were individuals Paul had unquestionably trained and poured his life into during his three-year ministry in the city of Ephesus (Acts 20:31). Paul was now prepared to conduct a pastors' conference for their edification.

A Pauline Pastors' Conference

In verse 18, Paul says to the Ephesian pastors that they knew how he lived while he was among them. Aristotle in his *Rhetoric* provides three modes of proof used to persuade the hearer: *logos, pathos,* and *ethos.* According to Aristotle ethos is the most significant of the three while logos provides content and pathos furnishes passion. Ethos offers a portrait of character. Paul reminded these leaders that they knew him (employing ethos), for they had three years to observe the way he lived while he was among them (Acts 20:31).

In verse 19, the apostle shares with them that above everything else he has been a servant and has attempted to live his life according to the Christ model. He served the Lord with all humility—that is, he served the Lord and experienced humiliation as a result. This is what Christ did; he condescended and took on the form of a servant and was obedient unto death, even death on the cross—the most ignominious and shameful form of death in that day (Phil 2:8). Like his Lord, Paul experienced great humiliation during his ministry (2 Cor 11:24–29). Paul enumerates the humiliation he faced in the midst of false brothers and in the face of stoning and shipwrecks. Paul also says he served the Lord with tears. He mentions tears as well in verses 31 and 37. Tears! Jesus was a man of sorrow and acquainted with grief. He wept over the wall of Jerusalem (Luke 19:41). He wept in the Bethany community (John 11:35). In fact tears represent a language God understands. In this case Paul's tears symbolized the liquid love he shed for the Ephesian pastors. Paul also brings attention to the fact that his serving took place in the midst of plots set by the Jews to destroy him. His Lord also faced plots during His three-year ministry. The Pharisees, Sadducees, and other groups and leaders plotted to destroy Jesus. Paul was not exempt from this clandestine activity and narrowly escaped several times, always by the grace of God.

From Profitable to Palatable

In verse 20, Paul has an *Acts 20:20 vision* for these Ephesian pastors. He reminds them that he held back nothing that was profitable for them. In 2 Timothy 3:16–17, Paul proclaims that "all Scripture is inspired by God and is *profitable* for teaching, for rebuking, for correcting, for training in righteousness, so that the man of God may be complete, equipped for every good work" (emphasis added). Paul knew that even though Scripture is *profitable* for the believer, it will not always be *palatable* initially to the believer. I remember eating foods as a young boy that my mother believed were *profitable* for my health, but they were not *palatable* initially to my appetite. Boiled okra was one of those foods. I made a commitment to myself that once I became grown, I would not eat boiled okra any more. However, my mother kept feeding boiled okra to me because she believed it was *profitable*, and eventually I developed a taste for it so that it finally became *palatable*. Today it is one of my favorite foods. The whole counsel of God may offer truths that are *profitable* but are not *palatable* initially. However, ministers must continue to present these truths to believers in hopes that the *already of the profitable* will be united with the *not yet of the palatable*. Paul also says in verse 20 that he proclaimed the truth to these leaders and taught them publicly and privately. Paul had spent three years in Ephesus ministering to the people. Two years were spent in the hall of Tyrannus teaching and training believers (Acts 19:9–10). He also went from house to house. It was not until the fourth century AD that the church began to meet in edifices or church buildings. Priscilla and Aquila used their house as a meeting place for the church (1 Cor 16:19). In Acts 20:7–12, Paul was preaching in a house where a young man named Eutychus went to sleep and fell out of the third-story window only to be revived by Paul through the power of God.

Contemporarily speaking, the hall of Tyrannus may represent the academy today, and the "house to house" system could symbolize the place where the church meets for worship. There must always be a connection between the academy and the church congregation, the lectern and the pulpit. Paul was comfortable preaching and teaching in both locations. Theology must be preachable. Theology must always be in service of the church. Paul was able to live between the hall of Tyrannus (Acts 19:9–10) and the houses in which people live (Acts 20:20) because his theology was portable and profitable. When ministers show care for the souls of the people in the congregant's house during the week, then individuals will show care for the sermon in the church house on Sunday morning.

Two Components of Paul's Proclamation: Repentance and Faith

In verse 21, Paul offers two components of his preaching and teaching ministry: repentance and faith. He has been preaching the gospel to both

Jews and Gentiles. Paul had stated, "I am not ashamed of the gospel, because it is God's power for salvation to everyone who believes, first to the Jew, and also to the Greek" (Rom 1:16). Christ is the one mediator between God and humans (1 Tim 2:5) and has the only name that heaven recognizes for salvation (Acts 4:12). Those who deny Christ and turn toward another for salvation are excluded. Salvation does not reside in any other person, only in Christ. The gospel renounces pluralism as an alternate route to redemption. Jesus Himself said, "I am the way, the truth, and the life. No one comes to the Father except through Me" (John 14:6).

Paul preached *repentance toward God*. Repentance, or *metanoia*, is a change in direction. It is a symbolical cutting off of one's head and replacing it with another head—that is, a changing of the mind. One of the great pictures of repentance in the Bible is seen through the experience of the prodigal son who came to himself, returned home, and repented in the presence of his father for his actions and behavior.

Another component of Paul's proclamation was *faith in our Lord Jesus Christ* (Acts 20:21). Paul did not advocate mere intellectual faith. He preached faith as connected to an object. One cannot have faith in faith but must have faith in God. This is saving faith. Believers are saved by faith through grace alone, but grace is never alone, for real believing faith results in action. Paul refers to the work of faith when he mentions the reputation of the Thessalonian Christians (1 Thess 1:3).

Living Between Mystery and Revelation: Paul's Theologia Crucis and Theologia Gloriae

In verse 22, Paul acknowledges that he does not definitively know what will happen to him. Here is a man who was caught up to the third heaven and received surpassing revelations beyond human experience. Yet he does not specifically know what will happen to him. He lived between mystery and revelation, between the known and the unknown.

In verse 23, the only thing Paul is aware of is that the Spirit has testified, as Paul makes his way to Jerusalem, that imprisonment and persecution await him. Here is an instance of the inextricable relationship between a theology of the cross and a theology of glory. Martin Luther indicted the scholastics because of their theology of advancement, promotion, and attainment—a theology of glory. For Paul and Luther real Christianity is a marriage between *theologia crucis* and *theologia gloriae*. This is what Jesus meant in Luke 24:26,

"Didn't the Messiah have to *suffer* these things and enter into His *glory*?" (emphasis added). Paul himself states in Philippians 3:10, "My goal is to know Him and the power of His resurrection and the fellowship of His sufferings, being conformed to His death." In light of these truths, prosperity theology is insufficient and inadequate. Instead of prosperity theology we need adversity theology. The whole counsel of God reminds us that *glory* and *gory*, *laughter* and *lamentation*, *singing* and *sighing*, and *feasting* and *fasting* go together. *What God has joined together let no one put asunder!*

In verse 24, Paul displays his irrepressible call and his indomitable spirit in relation to the ministry. He admits that none of the conflicts and spiritual warfare he has faced has moved him to the point of giving up: "I count my life of no value to myself." Although at times disappointed, mistreated, and abused, nothing moved Paul to the point of resigning the ministry. On one occasion some of the at-large disciples heard the teaching of Jesus and stated that it was hard and chose to walk with him no more (John 6:60, 66). Jesus turned to his twelve disciples and asked them if they would also leave. Peter responded by saying, "Lord, who will we go to? You have the words of eternal life" (John 6:67–68). The Christian minister in declaring the whole counsel of God must be resolved to the point of nonresignation. Paul was more concerned about the gospel than he was about the grave: "But I count my life of no value to myself" (Acts 20:24). He knew that ultimately his enemies could do nothing with him. They could not bring him to the point of resignation by hiding him in a jail cell where he would never see the light of day *because* his life was already hidden in Christ. They could not bring him to the place of resignation by killing him *because* he was already crucified with Christ. They could not bring him to the position of resignation by burying his body in an unmarked tomb *because* one day he would be resurrected by his Lord. Nothing moved Paul. All he wanted to do was to finish his course with joy. That is what his Master did. *Tetelestai*—"It is finished!" (John 19:30). This is what the Lord said from the cross. Paul would later say to his son Timothy, "I have fought the good fight, I have *finished* the race, I have kept the faith" (2 Tim 4:7, emphasis added). Paul not only wanted to finish his course, but he wanted to conclude it with joy. Once again this is what his Lord accomplished. The Hebrew writer describes Jesus' temperament when facing the cross: "Who for the joy that lay before Him endured a cross" (Heb 12:2).

Paul as Ezekiel's Watchman

Paul acknowledges that the ministry he carried on was one he had been called into, "the ministry I have received from the Lord Jesus" (Acts 20:24). The apostle Paul did not initially volunteer for this ministry, nor did he assume it by heredity or genealogy; he received it from the Lord Jesus Christ. Hear him saying in Acts 26:26, "Since this [referring to his calling] was not done in a corner!" Paul described his call as one "to testify of the gospel of God's grace" (Acts 20:24). There can be no gospel without grace; and yet grace is preceded by law (John 1:17). The law serves as a mirror to show us our sin; however, the law which came by Moses is transcended by the grace that comes through Jesus Christ. Grace points us to a fountain that is filled with blood in which we can lose all our guilt and stain. In fact the law serves as a tutor or trainer that leads us to Christ (Gal 3:24). For Christians, where sin abounds, grace does much more abound.

In verse 25, Paul notifies these Ephesian pastors that they will not see his face again. This notice brings them great sadness and causes them to weep (Acts 20:37). They had been around Paul for three years, listening to him preach the reign of God in the realm of his people. Paul was posturing them to carry on the kingdom of God in his absence.

In verse 26, Paul admits that he is innocent of the blood of all persons because he had held back nothing from them that was profitable. He had presented the whole counsel of God without compromise. Paul is undoubtedly in conversation with Ezekiel's watchman metaphor (Ezek 3:17–19; 33:1–6). The task of a watchman was to stand on the wall and look out over the horizon and warn the militia and residents inside the city walls when the enemy was approaching. In the event that the militia and the people did not heed the watchman's warning and suffered defeat and death by the hands of the invading army, the watchman was cleared of any responsibility for the demise of the city. As a Christian minister Paul did not hold back but shared the words he received from God for three years in Ephesus.

In verse 27, Paul makes this confession: "I did not shrink back from declaring to you the whole plan [counsel] of God." The "whole counsel of God" is that *concept that unites and ties together every passage of Scripture so that it relates to the overall plan and comprehensive purpose of God revealed in the Bible through the Holy Spirit in order to magnify Jesus Christ.*

In verses 28–30, the apostle Paul is persuaded that the Christian minister must watch three people groups. First, the Christian minister must watch himself: "Be on guard for yourselves" (Acts 20:28). Paul has already stated in Acts 20:18, "You know . . . how I was with you the whole time." The lips of the minister must be matched by his life, his beliefs by his behavior, his doctrine by his deeds. We must watch ourselves!

Second, the Christian minister must watch over the flock: "And for all the flock that the Holy Spirit has appointed you to as overseers" (Acts 20:28). The task of the Christian minister is ultimately to feed the flock and to care for its members. A shepherd who fails to feed the flock has actually renounced the ministry. Notice that the flock does not belong to the shepherd or the pastor; it belongs to God. Peter reminds pastors to labor, "not lording it over those entrusted to you, but being examples to the flock" (1 Pet 5:3). We are God's people and the sheep of God's pasture (Ps 100:3). We must watch over the flock, the flock over which the Holy Spirit has made us overseers. We may be called by churches, but we are appointed by the Spirit to oversee the flock that has been purchased by the blood of Jesus Christ (1 Pet 1:18–19).

Third, Christian ministers are to watch for would-be intruders outside the flock. These are those who bring false teaching into the congregation. Christian ministers are also to watch inside of the flock for false teachers who seek to draw away disciples after them (Acts 20:30). The apostle Paul admonished his young protégé Timothy to be on the lookout for false teachers like Hymenaeus and Philetus, who had wandered away from the truth and said the resurrection had already taken place, for they were destroying the faith of some (2 Tim 2:17–18).

Paul's concern is expressed in these terms, "I know that after my departure savage wolves will come in among you, not sparing the flock" (Acts 20:29). There lies within these three "watching imperatives" the task of *catechesis*; we are to feed the church of God from the Word of God. This is what the shepherd does in Psalm 23:2: "He makes me lie down in green pastures." The people of God often stray because they are tired of being fed brown grass; they want to eat from green pastures. Sometimes pastures look green only to contain poisonous, heretical vegetation. There is also the task of the *polemic*. In Psalm 51:8 the psalmist cries out to God, "Let the bones You have crushed rejoice." The Christian minister must reprove and rebuke in order that the congregation may rejoice. The third imperative is that of *apologetics*. The shepherd in Psalm 23:4 uses a rod to defend the sheep from animals of prey. The task of the Christian minister is to defend orthodoxy against heterodoxy and truth against falsehood.

In verse 31, Paul states that for three years he has been warning the Ephesian pastors about the encroachment of false doctrine. The contemporary Christian minister must prepare the church and the academy to recognize false doctrine for themselves, thereby preparing the church for the minister's absence while the minister is still present. Oftentimes the strength of one's ministry is seen in its longevity after the Christian minister has departed through retirement or death.

In verse 32, Paul commends these Ephesian pastors to God and to the Word of his grace. He knows the Word is able to edify them and to give them an inheritance among those who are sanctified and separated for the work of God.

In verses 33–35, Paul virtually confesses that he has not been a *prophet* for *profit*; he was not in the ministry for gain (Acts 20:33). Rather he was in the ministry to give. He chose to labor with his own hands in the tent-making industry so he could support himself, support others who worked with him in ministry, and support the weak (Acts 20:34). He was in ministry to give and patterned his ministry after his Lord, who said, "It is more blessed to give than to receive" (Acts 20:35).

CONCLUSION

In verses 36–38, Paul finished the pastors' conference with the Ephesian leaders. He knelt down and prayed with them (Acts 20:36). He and the Ephesian pastors wept, and they embraced and kissed him (Acts 20:37). This is one of the most spiritually intimate scenes in all of Scripture. Here are men who love God, sharing their hearts because they love one another in Christ. Paul and these pastors wept freely. Christian ministers must not be known only for their toughness in the way they hold to the truth but also for their tenderness and tears in the way they relate to believers. The Ephesian pastors wept most of all because of Paul's words that they will see his face no more (Acts 20:38). They then accompanied him to the ship. Eschatologically speaking, while Christian ministers and their constituency *meet to part*, in reality *they part to meet*. The blessed hope for all believers is that one day they will see his face (Rev 22:4).

O, I Want to See Him
As I journey through this land, singing as I go.
Pointing souls to Calvary, through the crimson flow.

Many arrows pierce my soul, from without, within.
But my Lord leads me on, through Him I will win.
O, I want to see Him; look upon His face.
There to sing forever of His saving grace.
On the streets the glory let me lift my voice.
Cares all past, home at last, ever to rejoice.[5]

---

[5] R. H. Cornelius, "O, I Want to See Him," public domain.

Leadership Lessons from David S. Dockery

Conviction and Courage

Gene C. Fant Jr.

If you think you are leading, but no one is following you, you are merely taking a walk.[1]

L eaders typically find themselves in positions of authority that force
people to follow them whether willingly or mandatorily, but transformational leadership is more a function of a person than a position. Even someone who has a leader's title can look to the rear one day and realize that no
one is actually following. The reverse can be true as well: someone who has
no formal title can glance behind and realize that an entire line of people is
following.

For the latter leader the epiphany that discovers, "Wow! I'm a leader!"
is one that carries great temptation. In one direction lurk egomania and the
so-called will to power, as Friedrich Nietzsche once phrased it. For Christ
followers this direction leads toward devastation and chaos and is paved with
anxiety and paranoia, the fear of losing power. In the other direction lies the
path of the servant who leads selflessly and influentially. This path is illumined
by the confidence that grows from conviction and courage.

---

[1] John C. Maxwell and many others have employed this quotation, often attributed to an
"ancient Afghan proverb," accessed January 14, 2014, http://johnmaxwellon
leadership.com/2012/08/07/are-you-really-leading-or-are-you-just-taking-a-walk.

Convictional leaders will always find followers whose own passions enable them to seek dedication and excellence. Followers will queue up behind courageous leaders who are willing to ignore their own fears and pursue significance. Courage rooted in conviction rather than recklessness is rare, but it is one of the most effective traits of the God-honoring leader.

CALLING PRODUCES CONVICTION

Former CEO of Chick-fil-A Jimmy Collins has written about his experiences working with company founder Truett Cathy in *Creative Followership: In the Shadow of Greatness.*[2] In Collins' view leadership is not about seeking leadership; it is about finding someone worth following and learning to be a follower. His point is that people will always follow others who are following a great leader. Leadership begins, for Collins, with an invitation to serve a leader ("boss," as he terms it for his business leaders).

Collins goes so far as to recount how he had worked on some projects for Cathy, and one conversation ended up leading to a job offer. When the opportunity came, he wavered a bit (read the book to see why) but eventually decided to cast his lot with the visionary entrepreneur, leaving behind his own business and risking everything to see where the opportunity led.

One of the most difficult tasks for an emerging leader is discerning how to formulate and demonstrate appropriate ambition. Our society casts a jaundiced eye toward ambition because it so easily perverts into egocentrism. Too often "insatiable ambition" is a redundant phrase that occurs when someone has turned it inward, impelled by one's selfish desires. Appropriate ambition, however, is perhaps better understood as a passion for excellence and for fulfilling the responsibilities with which one has been entrusted. Such an ambition to serve, not to advance, is attenuated externally to serving not only those within the sphere of leadership but to serving the one who has provided the trust.

Imagine how transformational it would be for Christians who find themselves in a position of leadership to be ambitious to serve God and others? Instead of being ambitious to *be* something, one would be ambitious to *do* something, to subordinate our lives to God's calling on our lives.

Collins emphasizes that his following Cathy worked precisely because both of them were actually following Christ. If Collins had not been a Christ

---

[2] Jimmy Collins, with Michael Cooley, *Creative Followership: In the Shadow of Greatness. My Journey to President of Chick-fil-A* (Decatur, GA: Looking Glass, 2013).

follower, the relationship would not have worked any better than if Cathy had not been a Christ follower. Both men saw their lives in the same terms as had the original disciples, who were called from their nets and their desks to follow the Master who gave them new tasks (see Matt 4, for example).

Understanding the concept of calling likewise allows us to shed the impulses we may have toward turf claims. In 1 Corinthians 3, Paul describes how we are "God's coworkers" (v. 9), an image that brings to sharp focus the image that we join God in his work; we work alongside God. Because we are working alongside him, at his invitation, any claims that we are "in charge" and, therefore, should receive credit are absurd. David, for example, was an amazing example of God's using a man to accomplish his purposes. Acts 13:36 says, "David, after serving his own generation in God's plan, fell asleep, was buried with his fathers, and decayed." This is not the language of "credit" or "resume building." This is the description of one who was called and who understood that calling is a platform for obedience.

When leadership is understood as obedience to a calling, everything changes. First, obedience imparts a particular kind of humility. Obedience is rooted in the concept of subordination, that one is beholden to someone else and is honor bound to fulfill that duty. Furthermore, obedient humility, the kind Christians should embrace, understands that our calling is not based on our innate talents or abilities but rather on those provided to us through God's providential will. We are not called because we are good but rather because God is great.

Obedient humility also eschews many of the trappings of leadership that can shorten a leader's tenure, from excessive perks and privileges to authoritarian excesses. Likewise obedient humility circumscribes tendencies that might lead to dishonesty and misrepresentations that are tempting when one is serving (or, more accurately, preserving) the self. Integrity, then, rests on a solid foundation of the Caller; God-obeying leaders are honest not because they want to be honest but rather because God is righteous and they are following him. When they cease to follow God's calling and honor God's authority, unrighteousness is quick to emerge in ever-increasing ways.

Just as importantly, a sense of calling produces conviction. *Conviction* may be another way of saying "resolute purpose." When we are called, we understand that we are given a task; we are called by someone to a specific work. No matter what the task may be—large or small, complicated or simple— wherever we find ourselves we are there because we are called to be there.

If a king sends an ambassador to negotiate an agreement, the ambassador's purpose must be resolute, representing the king's interests. The ambassador's own thoughts are irrelevant; the ambassador's fears or passions are likewise inconsequential. The ambassador's charge *from the king* is the basis for his convictions and his actions.

The connection between calling and conviction is a strong sense of duty: we represent the one who called us. Because we represent him, our choices are different. Anyone who has been in a high level of leadership knows that the position often overshadows the person who holds it. When I became an academic dean at Union University, I realized one day that my office door did not cite my name but rather just said, "Dean." When people saw me functioning, they saw the university and my academic unit, not me. In fact, when people referred to me, they rarely said, "Gene says this," instead declaring, "The dean says. . . ." In fact, when I tried to make decisions, I thought in the same terms, that I was not making the choices but instead that the organization somehow was working through me.

This made many choices, especially difficult ones, easier because I could analyze the options through the lens of institutional principles. I was not distracted by personal wishes; my preferences were irrelevant. I had convictions that were driven by the nature of my position; I was invited to the task by our president and both of us were, as Jimmy Collins said, following after the calling God had offered us. In the most difficult decisions I had to make, I found that my sense of courage to make the right, if unpopular, choices was increased exponentially as I stood on the principles that were inculcated by the calling that placed me in the position to make those choices. Instead of running the risk of being difficult and discouraging, I knew that God himself would empower and sustain my work for his glory.

CONVICTION YIELDS COURAGE

During my doctoral work I read widely on the leadership handbooks of the Renaissance, which are surprisingly relevant to our age. Baldesar Castiglione produced *The Book of the Courtier* in 1561, which became widely available in Europe and influenced humanists such as Shakespeare.[3] For Castiglione leadership (being a courtier, one who makes his living by serving princes) was a function of preparation and bearing. Leadership was a function

---

[3] Baldesar Castiglione, *The Book of the Courtier*, trans. Daniel Javitch and Charles S. Singleton (New York: Norton, 2002).

of doing, not being. In England the other significant work on leadership was the multiauthored sixteenth-century work *The Mirror for Magistrates*, which went through multiple editions and configurations. *The Mirror* was a series of poetic warnings against the errors rulers had made throughout history, including a dazzling array of luminaries such as King Arthur. *The Mirror* proposed that leaders are the sum total of their lack of errors of judgment.

These works are extensions, of a kind, of Machiavelli's *The Prince* (1532), which sought to eradicate the tissues of ideals that were accounted as advice for leaders but that paled before the vitality of raw power itself.[4] For Machiavelli the highest goal for a leader—indeed, the only goal—was power itself: its acquisition and its retention. This view was pragmatism of the worst sort, elevating the person over the institution and the position over those it would serve, at least nominally.

Twenty-first century culture tends to affirm views that are rooted in a materialistic worldview. Leadership is a function of ego and ambition. It is a vision of what could be, primarily directed toward the leader and only secondarily toward those who are led. What is good for the leader is, by definition, good for those who follow.

The problem with this approach to leadership is that it is corruptive, as Lord Acton famously noted. This means any kind of leadership that seeks after the self will constantly be fighting against being in decline. The will to power is a dynamic force; but once power is established, the basic laws of entropy and the fallen nature of this world mean that will is replaced with fear of the loss of power and position.

The dominant motivation for too many leaders is fearfulness. What if a major donor disagrees with a decision? What if a subordinate overshadows me? What if I stumble and people notice? Perhaps the most common fear is that of being caught not knowing something and appearing to be full of hot air. All too often this approach to leadership produces weak leaders and even weaker organizations.

For the Christian leader the first step is a conviction about the right order of the universe and one's place in that order. God is God. We are human. We are subordinate. God has chosen to reveal himself in Christ, in the Scriptures, and in the created world. When we operate out of a proper foundational conviction about major issues, we are equipped to seek the sound of God's

---

[4] Machiavelli, *The Prince and Selected Discourses*, trans. Daniel Donno (New York: Bantam, 1966).

applause rather than that of any group of persons. We seek the ultimate reward of the Christ follower: "Well done good and faithful slave" (Matt 25:21).

Albert Mohler has noted, "Convictional leaders propel action precisely because they are driven by deep convictions, and their passion for these convictions is transferred to followers who join in concerted action to do what they know to be right. And they know what is right because they know what is true."[5] Such leaders are passionate about justice, particularly that which is directed toward God himself.

We see this modeled in young David of the Old Testament. When the Philistines and Goliath were taunting the God of Israel (1 Samuel 17), David was incensed and took a bold stance where he defended God in the face of nearly certain death. His convictions overflowed into courage.

Courage is a sign of incredible integrity, which is, perhaps, why it is as scarce as it is. Stephen L. Carter writes that integrity "requires three steps: (1) discerning what is right and what is wrong; (2) acting on what you have discerned, even at personal cost; and (3) saying openly that you are acting on your understanding of right and wrong."[6] This model of integrity lies at the intersection of conviction and courage; it does not merely encourage courage, it *dictates* that courage be the active overflow of convictions about what is right and wrong and why something is one way or the other.

Courage is mere decoration when times are peaceful. But in crises true courage is readily evident and is necessary to prevent quailing in the face of adversity. Moreover genuine courage is incredibly rare. It is found only in the footsteps of Christ's calling over our lives.

PRINCIPLE YIELDS PREDICTABILITY

Organizational leadership practices tend to emphasize strategic planning and clarity of communication as primary markers of effectiveness. Strategic planning allows everyone in the organization to row in the same direction, heading toward a common destination. Planning streamlines decision-making because it provides everyone with a common set of criteria on which to evaluate opportunities and challenges. Clarity of communication constantly reminds everyone what the goals are and how they are being achieved.

---

[5]   Albert Mohler, *The Conviction to Lead: 25 Principles for Leadership that Matters* (Minneapolis: Bethany House, 2012), 26.

[6]   Stephen L. Carter, *Integrity* (New York: Basic, 1996), 7.

Yum! Brands CEO David Novak says that he once asked the legendary CEO of General Electric, Jack Welch, what he would do differently if he had to do things over. Welch responded by saying, "I wish I would've talked to our people more about what kind of company I envisioned us to be . . . what our values were and what we really stood for."[7]

In too many organizations, however, the overarching principles that guide everyone's work are either economic (How can I earn more?) or power based (How can I advance my position or maintain my political capital?). This means the organization does not possess principle, but rather its members all possess principles that are too easily conflicting and even confounding.

For Christ followers conviction projects itself into principles, which are able to be operationalized by leaders. Principle is the opposite of polling, where leaders solicit opinions and discern what opinion will either gain the most followers or will rankle the fewest feathers.

Opinion differs from insight. The wise leader will gather insight from the community, where people share their views or experiences that have been processed through overarching points of view. In a healthy organization everyone who offers insights will be aligned with the same point of view, one that has been cultivated by the leader to provide the clearest vision for the organization. Insights are organizationally oriented; they view everything in ways that will allow the group to thrive. Opinions, however, are driven by self-centered considerations, mainly, "How will this affect me?"

Too often leaders spend time gathering opinions rather than insights. The larger issue, however, is that unless an organization is principled, and its leaders clarify, cultivate, and perpetuate its core values and convictions, little more than opinion can be offered.

For Christ followers principle is the overflow of thinking theologically about everything. Principle keeps things level, as theological foundations are the standards by which principles must be judged.

At my university, for example, we have many students, faculty, and staff who travel internationally on mission trips, study-abroad programs, and for personal enrichment. A number of years ago, we realized the risks that are being undertaken by these trips, and we began to think about how we as an institution might prepare for mitigating these risks. At one meeting we had a kind of "spit-balling" session where we brainstormed and came up with a long

---

[7] David Novak, *Taking People with You: The Only Way to Make BIG Things Happen* (New York: Portfolio/Penguin, 2012), 5.

list of ideas and scenarios for planning. Soon, however, we realized that some of the items were inconsistent or even contradictory. We took a step back and determined that we did not need opinions; we needed to begin with principles that could guide the insights we would then gain. Our president, David Dockery, drafted for us a document that explored a theological foundation for our work, what the rationale was for Christians who travel, what kinds of risks are acceptable, and what kinds of responses we might offer to various kinds of challenges. The theology produced the principles, which then governed our discussions and decisions.

The beauty of this plan was that our discussions were now predictable. We knew, or at least could anticipate, what others might offer as insights. Predictability meant that our empathy was heightened because we could put ourselves in others' shoes and imagine what they might think or feel.

Predictability is the result of much hard work. Certainly an organization can become too predictable to the point that it is tradition bound and irrelevant to its context, but predictability is what makes the world work. In the most literal sense, the laws of physics favor predictability, for that which is unpredictable is also unstable. Imagine what driving would be like if the laws of physics varied at will, where there was no way of knowing what direction the steering wheel might turn?

Many organizations, however, operate with unsettled internal physics. No one knows where things are headed or exactly how they will reach whatever destinations have been hazily outlined. Followers often have no idea how a leader might react to an idea or respond to an opportunity. A leader who is unprincipled might take an ethical stance on one issue and display a moral failing on another equally important matter. A leader might articulate one vision one month and operationalize another the next. In the end everyone associated with the organization receives a kind of painful whiplash.

A lack of principle makes planning extremely difficult. When an organization loses a sense of its foundational principles, decision-making is next to impossible. Instead of tending to core functions, leaders at all levels find themselves pursuing almost anything *other* than their actual duties, chasing after novelty. Sergio Zyman warns against this kind of chaos, reminding leaders that without core principles "a huge amount of time and money goes into exploring and developing every new idea that comes down the pike. . . . A lot of really dopey ideas don't get weeded out when they should."[8]

Unpredictability is expensive in that efficiency is lost quickly. It leads to staff turnover. It generates a sort of free-floating anxiety that haunts every decision that is made and ultimately yields an overarching sense of pessimism for the organization. Management guru Jim Collins has observed that in the latter stages of an organization's life "confusion and cynicism" become the order of the day:

> People cannot easily articulate what the organization stands for; core values have eroded to the point of irrelevance; the organization has become "just another place to work," a place to get a paycheck; people lose faith in their ability to triumph and prevail. Instead of passionately believing in the organization's core values and purpose, people become distrustful, regarding visions and values as little more than PR and rhetoric.[9]

In every circumstance, pessimism is poison to a culture of any size. Optimism, genuine based-in-reality optimism, is the only antidote that can save the day.

ORTHODOXY YIELDS OPTIMISM

In theology predictability functions in the form of orthodoxy. If you wish to know what Baptists or Lutherans believe, you can predict the answer based on their statements and confessions of faith. Christianity's views on the incarnation are predictable because the church has wrestled with those views and has invoked the Scriptures and subsequent traditions in ways that have helped all Christians in all times understand what is acceptable and what is not. Orthodoxy is a consistent expression of the faith.

While the Scriptures are authoritative, the various great confessions of the church have provided us with means of articulating exactly what the Bible means for various cultures, languages, and eras. In these documents we learn about the Trinity, the incarnation, the church, and last things; and from these statements we are able to define orthodoxy.

---

[8] Sergio Zyman, *Renovate Before You Innovate: Why Doing the New Thing Might Not Be the Right Thing* (New York: Portfolio/Penguin, 2004), 8.
[9] Jim Collins, *How the Mighty Fall: And Why Some Companies Never Give In* (New York: HarperCollins, 2009), 101.

The Apostle's Creed, for example, has guided Christians in their thinking for almost two millennia. While the creed is theological, it is also a guide for how Christians should think about this world as well. For example, its theological truths exude a strong sense of teleology (end, purpose, or goal) for our lives. An effect of this teleology should be an overwhelming sense of optimism. Not only does our world owe its existence to God, but in Christ we have a righteous Judge who will vindicate the righteous. In spite of death and chaos, Christ remained victorious: "he rose again from the dead"; "he ascended into heaven"; "he shall come to judge the quick and the dead"; and because of this, we ourselves shall enjoy "forgiveness of sins" and "the resurrection of the body."

As the psalmist said, "Even when I go through the darkest valley, I fear no danger, for You are with me" (23:4). One of the great promises of the Christian life is that we are not promised deliverance from trouble, but rather we are promised that we will not be alone in our problems. Providence is a tremendous comfort to those who believe in the promise of the Comforter (John 14:16 KJV), as are the promises of Romans 8, that God will redeem all circumstances for his purposes.

Such comfort means Christ followers cannot ultimately be pessimistic. If we are to remain true to orthodoxy, we must be optimistic because we know God's power and glory transcend anything this world might throw our way. This optimism is not bound by this world but may find its ultimate confirmation in the next, such that we look forward to the consummation of God's creation beyond this life.

For leaders this promise of an optimistic resolution to challenges is comforting, or at least it should be. Leaders know the underbelly of an organization. As the saying goes, they see the sausage being made, butchering and all, and know that what others might see is not always the result of sunlight and fresh breezes. They know the real challenges to organizational existence or the dismal sides to interpersonal conflicts. Leaders cannot, however, focus on these realities, for they do not define the sum total of reality.

I would add, however, that orthodox optimism likewise understands the nature of reality, that difficulties will come. This means an optimistic leader must be a prepared leader: because we know storms will come, we need to have plans in place that will allow us to walk through those times. By dealing with them in advance, when we are not emotional or exhausted, we are able to engage the darkest parts of life's vicissitudes with positive responses. In fact, a prepared leader is able to be an optimistic leader precisely because when the sky is at its darkest, he has already picked up a flashlight to illumine his work.

I once heard former New York City mayor Rudy Guiliani say that optimism is the most critical trait for a leader to possess. In the wake of September 11, when he was pressed to lead in an incredible crisis, he knew that the least bit of pessimism would amplify the city's anxieties. Within minutes of the tragedy, he made clear that his office was taking care of business and that there was a plan for dealing with the aftermath.

Optimism is easy when one is in a peaceful meadow or is innocent of the most vicious parts of our world. Optimism, however, is most necessary precisely when it is most difficult to project. And it must be the default tone of any leader who has embraced the orthodox Christian faith. We know that in the end history always moves with a teleological purpose and that Christ wins, no matter what the battle might be.

A CASE STUDY: JACKSON, TENNESSEE, FEBRUARY 5, 2008

While the purpose of this present volume is not the study of David S. Dockery's leadership *per se*, a bit of space must be provided in these pages to address the elephant in the room: the tornado of 2008. Few events in American higher education are more worthy of study in the context of leadership than that of the natural disaster that threatened to shutter a 175-year-old institution.

In 2002, I joined the faculty of Union University in Jackson, Tennessee, arriving from a sister Baptist institution and relishing the opportunity to work in the vibrant learning community President Dockery had cultivated. From the beginning of my service, I was impressed with Dockery's leadership and counted myself blessed to have a front-row seat from which to see how his convictions were seamlessly integrated into his day-to-day work.

I had heard stories (some whispered and some nearly legendary) of Dockery's courage, of turning down tempting financial gifts that would have demanded watering down the institution's mission, of standing up to naysayers gracefully, of casting a breathtaking campus master plan that all but elicited jeers but somehow was realized during his time in office. I knew up close how patient and generous he was in dealing with challenges.

I understood quickly that everything that happened on campus was rooted in deep theological convictions. How do we handle the risks of international travel with students and mission trips? By crafting a theology of risk management, of course. How do we navigate the thornier issues of faith and culture? By studying the history of the church and examining its theological arguments. How do we stand up to the steep anxieties of a rapidly changing academic environment and surrounding culture? By clinging to Providence and an orthodox understanding of our faith.

Early in his presidency Dockery, driven by these foundational principles, established the university's four core values: excellence driven, Christ centered, people focused, and future directed, which were accompanied by a detailed statement of faith. These foundational documents grew out of the theological convictions he had framed for the campus.

On February 5, 2008, at 7:02 p.m., an EF 4 tornado with 200 mph winds sliced through the heart of the campus. The dean of Union's School of Theology and Missions, Gregory Alan Thornbury, now president of The King's College, and I, at that time the dean of the College of Arts and Sciences, along with Dockery, had returned to campus as the funnel cloud was on campus and dashed to the scene of the tragedy within minutes of the strike. We saw disintegrated dorms, grabbed bloodied students, smelled raw sewerage gurgling from broken pipes, and heard the moans of the students who were trapped in the rubble.

At the edge of the worst devastation, we were grabbed by Aaron Lee Benson, the Art Department chairman, who bear-hugged Dockery and immediately enveloped him in prayer, thanking God for providing the campus with a godly leader who would now guide us to the other side of the crisis. Similar comments followed as we finalized our quick loop around campus. I was struck by how everyone immediately viewed Dockery as God's appointed worker for the task. It was clear that *he had been called* to that place for such a time as that.

Within an hour the emergency management director for the area had directed Dockery to the downtown communications center. Union's first lady, Lanese Dockery, asked me to drive him there, and I eagerly grabbed the car keys, driving us to that center, where we were joined by Tim Ellsworth, the director of media relations.

The night was a blur of phone interviews with national and local news networks, of rumor quashing, and of trying to avoid plunging into a state of shock.

At one point Dockery looked at us and said, "Do either of you have a calendar?"

Ellsworth pulled one up on his phone.

Curious, I asked, "A calendar?"

"Yes, we need to decide what day we will reopen."

Incredulous, I blurted out, "Sir, you do realize that we have lost all of our dorms and many of our classrooms. How on earth are we going to reopen any time soon?"

He looked me in the eyes and said, "We have to give out a reopening date tonight, at least a target, or we will lose our students, and we will never reopen the institution. We have students who need to graduate in May, who are going to seminary, law school, and medical school, who already have lined up jobs." He noted our need for at least the outline of a general plan, even while we worked on the details of something more specific.

As the first days of recovery moved forward, we were emboldened to make aggressive choices that were risky but that proved to be necessary to overcome the obstacles of time and logistics. U.S. Homeland Security director Michael Chertoff toured campus and was astounded by how quickly we had seized opportunities for renovation and innovation. I cannot express how many times our conversations on campus were sprinkled with the absolute conviction that the tornado was an opportunity for God to demonstrate his power. This widespread sense of *calling led to incredible courage* (not to mention stamina!).

From that point on the entire leadership team looked to our core values, the expression of our institution's foundational convictions, to guide our every thought. In spite of fifty-nine students hospitalized and hundreds more injured, with $25 million in damage, we reopened about two weeks later. In many meetings it was almost overwhelming to see how those four core values that had guided us on so many relatively minor decisions now steered us firmly as we were forced to make decisions reactively rather than proactively. We knew, however, that for the most part our overarching *principles were yielding breathtaking predictability.*

From our time in the command center forward, President Dockery communicated an incredible, contagious sense of optimism. People quickly developed a sense of expectation: God had been faithful during the tornado; what would he do in the wake of the tornado? As we moved from recovery to renewal, as our plan termed it, the campus moved quickly and resolutely. The hope that we would hold graduation on time, a radically irrational decision when it was announced, loomed on everyone's horizon as a goal toward which we would strive. Everyone pulled in that direction. Even as we reviewed construction plans for new dorms and began to build the following year's enrollment, we kept one eye fixed on graduation because of what that would symbolize. In May, on the same date that we had calendared pretornado, we gathered on the Great Lawn for the commencement services, marking the end of the semester and the beginning of a new day for the university. We had clung to Providence throughout those four months, and we saw vividly the fruits of how *orthodoxy produces optimism.*

Throughout the following summer many of us, exhausted from our work (I kept a record: I worked 179 hours the first ten days following the tornado) sat in our offices, sharing our experiences and the many ways we had seen God work in our midst. I recall one campus visitor (there were many, most of whom were drawn by overwhelming curiosity to see if it were true that we were rebuilding at an incredible pace) who said we had done in less than six months what on his public university campus would have taken at least five years. I loved to hear what then-vice president for Student Life Kimberly Thornbury called "Crazy, God Stories," of how things happened that made no rational sense. For my part I loved to tell people how a summer job I had during graduate school had prepared me to lead in converting a hotel into a dormitory in only a week (I had learned basic logistics and how to deal with moving large trucks through confined loading spaces at a dairy). Whenever anyone from off campus praised our work or tried to get us to brag about our emerging accomplishment, each of us found that the experience had provided us with a deep sense of humility that produced honesty: the event was not about human excellence but rather was about divine empowerment for God's ultimate glory.

In the wake of the tornado, many of us who served in leadership have had opportunities to share our experiences and to offer suggestions on disaster preparedness and crisis management on other campuses. I still have a difficult time making such presentations without choking up emotionally, but I also continue to give praise to God for his protection and for his providential calling of David Samuel Dockery to lead us through the challenges. We often joke that his parents named him aptly. David: the deeply courageous boy shepherd who defeated wild animals and giants and who sought after God's heart with firm conviction. Samuel: the prophet who was born to listen to God's calling on his life and served God's people strategically. What a pleasure and a blessing it has been to follow him as he followed after God.

Higher Education's Role in
Developing a Civil Society

Hunter Baker

O ne of the goals of political science is to validate theories of human action. For example, can we achieve a level of confidence that the chance of democratic nations engaging in war against one another is significantly lower than some of the alternatives (democracy v. authoritarian nation, authoritarian nation v. authoritarian nation, etc.)? There are many other interesting questions. Can the behavior of legislators be predicted under certain circumstances? Does a standing assembly act significantly differently from one that meets only every other year? In what ways will the presence of a professional army change the tenor of politics in a society as compared to one that relies on emergency conscription?

But some iron laws of politics are still more crucial and continue to elude our mastery despite their simplicity. One of those was considered to be of primary importance by the founding generation in the United States. It is this: *Freedom requires the exercise of virtue. If a people cannot govern themselves through the exercise of virtue, they will not be free.* The United States of America, as an ongoing project, is a dramatic and dynamic act of balancing law and virtue. The more virtuous the people, the less will we require the coercive and paternal action of the state. Indeed, the more we strive to be virtuous people, the more we will be "men with chests," as C. S. Lewis would have us, rather than mass men under the sway of elite "conditioners."[1] We will partici-

---

[1]   C. S. Lewis, *The Abolition of Man* (New York: Touchstone, 1996), 36–37, 75.

pate in bringing about the good society rather than simply drifting along with whatever state of affairs a set of masters determine to create.

The American Constitution is set up with an eye toward maintaining virtue and, therefore, freedom. One such way is to avoid tempting human beings with too much power. Rather than deal in the old question of "Who has the power?" the American founders sought to answer a more insightful inquiry: "How much power?" To that end the power of the American government is limited, checked, and balanced. The government created by the constitution is inherently a modest one, one that is suited to a free and virtuous people. But how could the founders ensure the people would be virtuous and therefore capable of being free? One important answer to that question was religion. The American founders were clearly heterogeneous when it came to the matter of religious orthodoxy (though not nearly so much so as we are today). We can find a motley collection of Christians, deists, and so-called "freethinkers" (a self-flattering designation) in the founding generation. But they were more united on the positive value of faith for building republican virtue. Washington's statement in his farewell address captures the sense of the founders well:

> *Of all the dispositions and habits which lead to political prosperity, religion and morality are indispensable supports.* In vain would that man claim the tribute of patriotism, who should labor to subvert these great pillars of human happiness, these firmest props of the duties of men and citizens. The mere politician, equally with the pious man, ought to respect and to cherish them. A volume could not trace all their connections with private and public felicity. Let it simply be asked: Where is the security for property, for reputation, for life, if the sense of religious obligation desert the oaths which are the instruments of investigation in courts of justice? And let us with caution indulge the supposition that morality can be maintained without religion. Whatever may be conceded to the influence of refined education on minds of peculiar structure, *reason and experience both forbid us to expect that national morality can prevail in exclusion of religious principle.*
>
> *It is substantially true that virtue or morality is a necessary spring of popular government. The rule, indeed, extends with more or less force to every species of free government.* Who that is a sincere friend to it can look with indifference upon attempts to shake the foundation of the

fabric?[2] (emphasis added)

In addition to religion, he pointed to the value of education:

Promote then, as an object of primary importance, institutions for the general diffusion of knowledge. In proportion as the structure of a government gives force to public opinion, it is essential that public opinion should be enlightened.[3]

When we consider the two quotes from the same source, we see Washington proclaiming that the nation should look to both religion and education for sustenance. It is especially interesting that he rejects the idea that "refined education" is adequate in itself to sustain virtue in the people. The United States of America would need a religious morality (based on Christianity) and educational institutions working together for the health of the republic.

CHRISTIAN CIVILIZATION

This thing Washington holds up as the realistic ideal is what we might call the civilization project. Specifically, it is the project of Christian civilization. David Dockery, president of Union University, has been one of the key colaborers in the project of Christian civilization since the late twentieth century, a period in which the project had declined precipitously. For a variety of reasons, Western elites from the late nineteenth century forward have embraced a liberal secularism free riding on the moral and social capital accrued by Christianity. Many universities (including the entirety of the Ivies) chose to forget about the project of preparing citizens for a place in Christian civilization. Dockery, among other key players before and since, understands the importance of the project and has aimed to realize it through a renewal of Christian colleges and universities old and new.

Christian civilization helped foster the emergence of a broad-based citizenship in America that was applauded by Alexis de Tocqueville when he visited the country in the nineteenth century. Need a thorny problem solved? The American national genius was that citizens would not wait passively for a solution from some central force but would rather organize themselves and tackle it immediately. They might opt for local government or for the

---

[2] "Washington's Farewell Address 1796," accessed May 29, 2014, http://avalon.law.yale.edu/18th_century/washing.asp.
[3] Ibid.

proliferating voluntary organizations they seemed to be so adept at creating. In this way Americans developed the civic muscle John Stuart Mill found so necessary to liberty. They acted upon their circumstances instead of waiting for circumstances to act upon them and developed the capacity for responsible and creative civic leadership.

America's churches and then the schools and churches worked in concert to train Americans for a largely new kind of life in the polis for many citizens. Gone was the old passivity and deference to rulers exhibited by mere subjects. In its place came the engaged role of the citizen. The Bible counsels Christians to obey their sovereigns, but one of the great differences of the new American life was that the people possessed a real share of the sovereignty. Sovereignty did not exist outside of them but within them and had to be used morally. While subjects need only obey, citizens have the weighty task of making a right use of freedom and the even more awesome challenge of deciding when to curtail wrong uses of freedom, which might be called license. Lest we give in to the temptation to follow some commentators who attribute this free citizenship primarily to secular impulses, it is good to remember, as Patricia Bonomi wrote in *Under the Cope of Heaven*, that the revolution occurred between the First and Second Great Awakenings in the United States.[4] It would be odd to think that the middle portion of that period was especially godless, as some have suggested.

The First Great Awakening is an important precursor to revolution. In that movement Christians began to shed themselves of intermediate ways of knowing God and opted for a more immediate experience of and relationship with Him. There is an active argument over whether the Revolutionary War was a just war and therefore met important requirements of Christian social doctrine. Leaving aside that question, it seems clear that Americans opted to take responsibility for their relationship to God en masse in the eighteenth century and subsequently moved to do the same with regard to sovereignty.

THE WEIGHT OF LIBERTY

One of the longstanding arguments about America has been over the degree to which it is a nation that holds liberty or equality closest to its heart. A senior professor friend of mine makes a little joke in providing his own answer. "Well," he says, "the answer is obviously equality. Look at our Equality

---

[4] Patricia U. Bonomi, *Under the Cope of Heaven: Religion, Society, and Politics in Colonial America* (New York: Oxford, 1986).

Bell and the beautiful Statue of Equality." His answer would be a nice riposte in a debate, but in a more scholarly vein we might look toward Benjamin Constant's famed 1819 essay, "The Liberty of the Ancients Compared with That of the Moderns." In the essay Constant's goal was to argue for a different kind of liberty than the one Jean Jacques Rousseau (a darling of the French Revolution) had promoted in his work.[5] Rousseau's ideal of liberty (ancient liberty, per Constant) amounted to something like true direct democracy in which citizens attempted to cast their vote in favor of the general will. Citizens were not urged to exercise their judgment with regard to the good so much as they were instructed to guess properly about the will of the group and then add their consent to it. Such a government would have tremendous power to regulate much of life. Constant argued for what he called "modern liberty." He hoped to limit the business of government to a circumscribed space in life and then to rely on citizens largely to govern themselves. Rather than accept the command to "obey and pay" in exchange for a government that promises to deliver happiness, Constant insisted that citizens should keep the work of gaining a happy life in their own hands. The following passage sums up his view nicely: "Political liberty, by submitting to all the citizens, without exception, the care and assessment of their most sacred interests, enlarges their spirit, ennobles their thoughts, and establishes among them a kind of intellectual equality which forms the glory and power of a people."[6]

Constant dreamed of a humane, reinforcing cycle between liberty and virtue. He hoped the responsibility of freedom would bring maturity and wisdom along with it. That cycle is possible, but it is far from guaranteed. There must be some legitimate source of virtue within the culture. Something must make morality more than a social construct to be embraced or disregarded on the basis of cynical, calculating interest.

GUINNESS'S WARNING

In *A Free People's Suicide*, Os Guinness questions whether the American way of life is sustainable. But when we talk about sustainability in this sense, the question is not whether America will keep its air clean, its water pure, or its forests lush. Guinness is interested in a deeper and more urgent question:

---

[5] Benjamin Constant, "The Liberty of the Ancients Compared with That of the Moderns, 1816," accessed May 29, 2014, http://www.uark.edu/depts/comminfo/cambridge/ancients. html.

[6] Ibid.

Will American freedom continue to thrive, or will it unravel as a result of its abuses?[7]

Guinness's question is driven by his view that "the greatest enemy of freedom is freedom."[8] A notion of substantive freedom organized around achieving a good life can devolve into nothing more than a selfish and atomistic freedom from constraint. Such freedom will not last because it cannot sustain itself. A freedom which is wholly negative in nature (freedom from control and constraint) is not enough. Freedom should also be constructive. Freedom to work. Freedom to plan. Freedom to invest. Freedom to make and keep commitments.

But something has changed for Americans after more than 200 years. Founding principles are ever in danger of appearing abstract and dry to younger generations. The earlier emphasis on character and virtue can seem quaint, outdated, and even obstructionist in the face of magnificent things that might be achieved with a combination of technology and the right expertise guiding government.

For Guinness, sustaining freedom requires a long perspective that surveys both the past and the horizon. In other words we should care about and learn from what our ancestors have done. At the same time we should be careful to respect the future and the people who will live in it. A people with virtue would take care to adopt that long view. We, on the other hand, do not appear to embrace it. Guinness points out that America has become the world's largest debtor by financing current consumption rather than infrastructure investment. He castigates the recent stimulus plan, noting that, "Never has one generation spent so much of its children's wealth in such a short time and with so little to show for it."[9]

There is little with which one can argue here. And Guinness correctly expresses alarm at the way we spend a great deal of time fretting over matters such as the machinations of terrorists and the rise of China as the next superpower while failing to perceive that the single greatest threat to America is not "wolves at the door but termites in the floor."[10] Former secretary of state Condoleeza Rice expressed a similar sentiment in her remarks at the recent Republican National Convention.

---

[7]   Os Guinness, *A Free People's Suicide: Sustainable Freedom and the American Future* (Downers Grove, IL: InterVarsity Press, 2012).

[8]   Ibid., 19.

[9]   Ibid., 26.

[10]   Ibid., 37.

We might be tempted to trust in American exceptionalism, but Guinness, lacking the emotional attachment of the natives, counsels against taking shelter there. As a subject of the British crown, he has seen that movie before. He does not deny that the United States has played an oversized role in the world for many decades now, but he eagerly debunks American belief that this country's blessed uniqueness will save it from the fate of other empires.[11]

If mystical American exceptionalism is not the answer, then what is? Guinness points to what he calls the golden triangle. The triangle consists of three points: freedom, virtue, and faith. Freedom requires virtue, which requires faith, which requires freedom. Almost anyone could agree that freedom depends on virtue and that faith requires freedom (what would be the value of a hard-coded robot praying?). Resistance kicks in at the idea that virtue requires faith. Guinness successfully demonstrates that the American founders held such an opinion in the spirit of sober political realism. But is it true? Guinness's answer on this point is powerful. He says, in brief, that we should let the atheists prove the point on a nationwide scale. Let them shoulder the responsibility of establishing some enduring foundation for virtue and take a break from their ceaseless efforts at deconstruction. He issues his challenge with confidence, noting that "no free and lasting civilization anywhere in history has so far been built on atheist foundations."[12]

The United States has benefitted tremendously from the ability of Christianity to underwrite the moral commitments of citizens, but as that once stronger consensus has become attenuated, we have observed the situation of which Phillip E. Johnson complained when he wrote that "we are arriving at an absurd condition that might be called libertarian socialism. Everyone has a right to live exactly as he or she pleases, but if something goes wrong, some abstraction called 'society' is to blame and must pay the bill for damages."[13] More bluntly, Johnson was saying that we live in a culture today in which we desire only the benefits of freedom and little to none of the responsibility. The *virtue* in the *virtuous* cycle is missing. Virtue has been trumped by desire.

We are in danger of abandoning a healthy and mature ideal of citizenship for a more infantile status as coddled subjects in a society living off eroding cultural and religious capital. One of the more notable characteristics of the

---

[11] Ibid., 175.

[12] Ibid., 120.

[13] Phillip E. Johnson, *Reason in the Balance* (Downer's Grove, IL: InterVarsity Press, 1998), 148.

people living in Aldous Huxley's *Brave New World* is that virtue is largely absent. Some people are clever, but it is understood that they have been bioengineered to be that way. To the extent anyone is really complimented, it is for being "pneumatic." In the context of the novel, the word *pneumatic* conveys a pleasing manly or womanly shape (muscles or curves). But the other meaning of pneumatic is "filled with air." It is unlikely that the double meaning was lost on Huxley. Huxley's future, one in which people are managed, manipulated, controlled, and satisfied with their lives (at least as long as they take their medication—"better to take a gramme than to give a damn"), is of a piece with Washington's warnings about the giant lacunae left by religion and morality.[14]

How do we restore the virtuous cycle intended by the architects of our democracy? Unsurprisingly, the answer, in part, is education. Guinness provides a brief apologia for the type of liberal education under siege in an America that takes an increasingly utilitarian and professionalized approach to learning. In the past Guinness has paid attention to the sociological logic of secularization and functional differentiation. He returns to that theme, noting that we have separated out various spheres of human activity, leaving them to run on their own, sometimes soulless logic. Though he doesn't put it this way, he hopes to see a transformation from independent, Weberian spheres to the Kuyperian alternative, which respects the individual excellence of various pursuits but still sees a higher unity for them under the lordship of Christ.[15]

Regrettably, Guinness's answer shows us the depth of our trouble. If we had the kind of society that cares about things like education for citizenship and the broader *paideia* of liberal education, we would not be trapped in a process of apparent decline. We are running in the opposite direction from the one Guinness recommends. At the primary and secondary levels, we are spending less time on history and civics in favor of the current emphasis on math and reading as our schools teach for standardized examinations to justify state funding. In our colleges pressures mount to add more hours to professional majors while cutting the total number of years required to graduate in order to reduce costs. The result will almost inevitably shrink the core curriculum, which is the one place we might gain a sense of unity between knowledge and virtue. Few want to argue against cutting the core because many see it as nothing more than a couple of unnecessary years standing in the way of

---

[14] Aldous Huxley, *Brave New World* (New York: Harper Perennial, 2006).
[15] Guinness, *A Free People's Suicide*, 192–93.

professional training. As our knowledge becomes narrower, we move further away from the ideal of real citizenship and closer to the political status of mere subjects.

We can only jump out of this track by becoming aware of our need for renewal. This is not some general feeling that will fall unbidden upon us. Rather, such a movement would come, as Guinness notes, in the way the Renaissance and the Reformation did, through a group of individuals pointing back to original sources.[16] *Ad fontes*. Renewal emerges through rediscovery of those things that spurred us on in the first place.

We have no guarantee that we will grow up to be faithful, strong, and free. Another path that lies before us is mediocre and manipulable. We can be free, or we can be managed.

WHAT'S A COLLEGE FOR?

In the United States the project of Christian civilization has largely been abandoned. Or perhaps more accurately we might say control of the civilization project went to the victors of a struggle. While the United States was founded through an alliance between serious Christians and enlightenment deists, over time the once healthy balance between Renaissance and Reformation has tipped strongly in favor of the former. Accordingly, partisans of the Enlightenment have managed to wrest control of the top culture-making institutions in American life, especially in the educational sector. The story is an old one and need not be rehearsed again here, but the fundamental goals of both higher education in the United States and of the professor class have changed in massive ways. Christian priorities have succumbed to the influence of the professions, of industry, of the political left, and of the cultural *avant garde*. Something similar nearly happened in the American church, as well. Had not the evangelicals emerged with vibrance in the wake of the fundamentalist controversy and had Vatican II been interpreted in a different fashion, the churches in America might have followed sister institutions in Western Europe into theological liberalism and *de minimis* impact among the people. So we still have a vital church (more or less affected by secularism and consumerism but still influential). What do we have when it comes to higher education by way of training leaders and citizens? What do we need?

In his highly stimulating 1957 book, *Landmarks of Tomorrow*, Peter Drucker examined higher education and several other critical societal levers.

---

[16] Ibid., 197.

Drucker, one of several Austrians who exerted a significant impact on thinking in the U.S., identified key questions faced by colleges and universities.
Will the employee be a technician, a simple master of technique, "a barbarian
in thrall to his tools," or will he be something more? Will he be interested
in the common good? Or rather will he be little more than a self-interested
individual looking to extract the maximum reward from the broader society
with the least personal investment possible?[17]

What about the institutions themselves? Are universities grounded in
such a way as to prepare students for a more responsible existence? *Landmarks
of Tomorrow* includes a disheartening story about a German university during
the early period of Nazi rule. When a new Nazi commissar was appointed to
head the institution, the professors turned obsequious. Would the biology department get more money? Would the law library be able to expand its hold-
ings? The answer was that there would be plenty of funds for those willing to
cooperate. The man who shared the account with Drucker said he feared the
same would be true of his own school where the focus is increasingly on nar-
row interests and pet projects.[18] Without a strong foundation, the university
becomes a multiversity in which the various players are primarily concerned
about what share of university resources they can command for their own initiatives. Students are just as capable of drawing a lesson from such a structure
of incentives as they are from eloquent lectures.

In a less sinister but still concerning vein, a half century later Yale
University's Anthony Kronman would write *Education's End: Why Our
Colleges and Universities Have Given Up on the Meaning of Life*. In the book,
he bemoaned the modern student's loss of interest in liberal arts and the
big questions that go along with them.[19] Around the same time the historian C. John Sommerville from the University of Florida would describe *The
Decline of the Secular University*. In that book he detailed the disappointment
of enlightenment liberals who had dreamed of dispensing with Christianity's
influence in the academy so as to replace it with their own only to find that
professors and students became increasingly oriented around careerist ob-
jectives.[20] Instead of good-bye Jerusalem and hello Athens, the result has

---

[17] Peter F. Drucker, *Landmarks of Tomorrow* (New York: Harper, 1959), 105.
[18] Ibid, 105–6.
[19] Anthony Kronman, *Education's End: Why Our Colleges and Universities Have Given Up on
the Meaning of Life* (New Haven, CT: Yale University Press, 2007), 32–33.
[20] C. John Sommerville, *The Decline of the Secular University* (New York: Oxford University
Press, 2006), 8.

been more like good-bye to Jerusalem *and* Athens and hello Wall Street and Silicon Valley. Technology and finance seem to shape the lives of Americans far more than philosophy and religion. Indeed, it could easily be argued that the decline of marriage and the rise of same-sex partnership is a consequence of one of the most transformative technologies of all time, the birth control pill. It decoupled sex from reproduction and marriage from sex. One could make the case that 5,000 years of history on same-sex marriage would have remained undisturbed without the unwinding influence of the pill.

Some would give up on higher education entirely. I recently listened to an interview between Peter Robinson and two highly successful venture capitalists in the technology sector: Peter Thiel and Andy Kessler.[21] Thiel is especially notable. He is a founder of PayPal and one of the original investors in Facebook. He gained notoriety a few years ago when he announced the Thiel Fellows program, which actually pays talented college-aged students $100,000 *not* to go to school. The purpose of the interview was to pit Thiel's growing pessimism about American innovation and our future against Kessler's optimism, but a question about higher education brought the two together. Both men seemed to endorse the notion that the only value of universities is as a sorting mechanism for intelligence. In other words, what is significant about a student having attended Harvard or Yale is that they had the ability to get into Harvard or Yale. That view implies perforce that the actual education received at either of those institutions is of no value. Better yet, the two men agreed, is to spend a few dollars on a good test of intelligence to identify the real talents among the young student population.

Is the Thiel-Kessler view an accurate appraisal of the good that comes to us from higher education? Is it just an overly expensive way to separate wheat from chaff? What's a college for?

ANSWERING THE QUESTION

I have a dream for a unique advertising campaign for Union University where I work. Each ad would feature an image of one of our students. Either above or below the image would be a statement that would obviously apply to the student pictured. "Believes in absolute truth." "Believes in keeping promises." "Works as unto the Lord." "Believes authority means something more

---

[21] *Uncommon Knowledge with Peter Robinson*. Podcast interview (September 13, 2013): "Peter Thiel and Andy Kessler on the State of Technology and Innovation," http://www.hoover.org/multimedia/uncommon-knowledge/156956.

than power." "Believes life has meaning." "Wants to leave a legacy." "Believes in the love of God." "Shows the love of God to others." "Doesn't marginalize the weak." "Embraces eccentric people rather than ostracizing them." "Believes the biggest questions in life have answers." I would love to send out hundreds of ads like that for my school.

These are the qualities I see in many of our students. More important, these qualities can grow within students during their years here at Union. With ACT scores well above average and good grades, our students represent a strong crop. Large numbers of them would perform well on the cheap tests of intelligence, which Thiel and Kessler seem to think would work as proxies for a college education. There was a time in America when it would have meant something more than intelligence to be "a Harvard man" or "a Yale man" or "a Radcliffe girl." It would have been understood that a certain code of gentlemanly or gentlewomanly behavior had been modeled for and imparted to the students. Some institutions have not given up on the bigger game. We are ambitious for more than the careers of our students. We are ambitious for their lives and their influence on the culture around them.

In Anthony Kronman's book mentioned above, there is an intriguing note in which he observes that while elite institutions such as his own have given up on discovering the meaning of life, the quest moves forward at Christian colleges and universities.[22] We are the ones undertaking the projects aimed at the reading of old books. We are the ones designing honors programs around primary texts and Socratic instruction. Kronman, a secular man, despaired a little to see the Christians gaining a monopoly over the work he wanted for his own people, but perhaps he will end up proud of what we do with it and how we revitalize the culture.

CONCLUSION

It sometimes seems that we have given up on our grand ideas of higher education. Increasingly we are urged to forget the large, overarching purposes and lofty visions. Go all-in on a strategy rooted in technique and vocation. Make education instrumental. Stop selling ends and major in means.

The problem is that despair about what education can do in the civilization project doesn't solve our problems. How will we prepare citizens for life in a democratic republic? How will we maintain true political ends worth

---

[22] Kronman, *Education's End*, 200.

pursuing? How will we preserve liberty if we fail in educating for virtue? What will happen if our stock of cultural capital is depleted?

The great Quaker philosopher D. Elton Trueblood is justly remembered for his metaphor of the cut flower civilization. His argument was simple. We have cut our civilization at the stem. Down in the soil is a rich mixture heavily seeded with the Judeo-Christian influence. It has made us more free, wise, and humane than we otherwise would have been. When you cut the flower (and maybe we did that decisively in the West sometime in the twentieth century), it continues to look beautiful and healthy. You can place it in water and continue to enjoy it. But in time it will wilt and eventually rot.[23]

The metaphor is not a hopeful one. But maybe there is hope. Maybe there can be new seedlings, a new work of planting and cultivation, a new time of growth. In any case Christians are not free to live without hope. We have the task of preserving our inheritance until such time as it can once again enjoy greater cultural expression. Union University, under the guidance of David Dockery, has taken its place in the church's vanguard and has sought to fortify that which has been deconstructed and depleted. Amid ruins there will be new birth and shoots of green. While others watch the old flower wilt, let us continue our work of gardening.

---

[23] D. Elton Trueblood, *The Predicament of Modern Man* (New York: Harper & Row, 1944), 59.

Imaging God Through Union with Christ

What We Can Learn from an Augustinian and Barthian Interpretation of Colossians 2:6–7 for the Future of Convictional Civility

Autumn Alcott Ridenour

Therefore, as you have received Christ Jesus the Lord, walk in Him, rooted and built up in Him and established in the faith, just as you were taught, overflowing with gratitude.

Colossians 2:6–7

The term "convictional civility" evokes two concepts as relevant for the Christian moral life in its aim at theological and cultural engagement. The first is conviction or confidence in one's theological identity. The second is "civil" engagement with one's neighbor, community, or even culture at large. Both concepts have biblical and historical roots beginning with the early disciples and remain throughout the Christian tradition's understanding of Scripture's injunction to be in the world but not of the world (John 17:11, 16). For two influential theologians, Augustine and Karl Barth, a strong theological identity provides the groundwork for engagement in the broader civil sphere.

Augustine redefines Cicero's original definition of a "commonwealth," "civitas" or communion of people from one that focuses on justice to one that focuses on persons united by common objects of love.[1] In other words, a commonwealth, *civitas*, or community is only as good as its loves. Likewise, Karl Barth and his theological colleagues of the Confessing Church challenge the German Christians in their famous 1934 Barmen Declaration to adhere to the gospel rather than be swayed by cultural Nazism.[2] Only insofar as the gospel remains central to the church's teachings does the church contribute and hold accountable the civil community and its moral values.

Thus, the heart of "convictional civility" begins with a theological identity rooted in our deepest loves and commitments. For Augustine love of God and neighbor consummated in Christ defines the moral life while for Barth obedience to the Divine Command that brings about fellowship with God and neighbor crystallizes ethical practice.[3] Thus, in order to understand a deeper consideration of convictional civility for the future of theological engagement, I turn to a constructive vision of Augustinian and Barthian theology in light of "Union with Christ" in its relation to Colossians 2:6–7.

Given David S. Dockery's own scholarly contribution as a biblical scholar and theologian, I here interpret Colossians 2:6–7 as theme verses for Union's 2012–2013 academic year in the spirit of Augustine and Barth who have significantly shaped not only theology but also the heart of moral living in a way that identifies with convictional civility. By turning to these figures within historical theology to interpret themes within this passage in the context of Colossians, I believe we will find the foundation and goal of the moral and spiritual life resides in union with Christ as pilgrims who are being *remade in the image* of Christ our Savior. In order to consider union with Christ as the heart of convictional civility, I will consider: (1) Christ as the image of God, (2) the goal of union with Christ as contemplation and action, and (3) the characteristics of being remade in the image of Christ.

---

[1] St. Augustine, *City of God* XIX.21, 24, trans. Henry Bettenson (London: Penguin Books, 1984), 881–83; 890–91; David Hollenbach, *The Common Good and Christian Ethics* (Cambridge: Cambridge University Press, 2002), 124–28; Oliver O'Donovan, *Common Objects of Love* (Grand Rapids: Eerdmans, 2002), 20–24.

[2] Karl Barth, "Theological Declaration of Barmen," May 1934, accessed July 7, 2014, http://www.sacred-texts.com/chr/barmen.htm.

[3] Augustine, *On Christian Teaching*, trans. R. P. H. Green (Oxford: Oxford University Press, 1997); *City of God*, trans. Henry Bettenson (London: Penguin Books, 1972); Karl Barth, *Church Dogmatics*, 4 vols. (Edinburgh: T&T Clark, 1960). Subsequent references will use CD.

CHRIST: THE IMAGE OF GOD

Therefore, as you have received Christ Jesus the Lord.

Colossians 2:6–7 begins saying, "Therefore, as you have received Christ Jesus the Lord," in a way that identifies the subject and motivation for the moral life as the person of Jesus Christ. The conjunction "therefore" signifies a previous passage in which the preeminence of Christ is described in Colossians 1:15–20. The Pauline text describes Christ as "the image of the invisible God, the firstborn over all creation. For everything was created by Him, in heaven and on earth, the visible and the invisible, whether thrones or dominions or rulers or authorities—all things have been created through Him and for Him" (Col 1:15–16). This passage proved central throughout the early Christological debates regarding the divinity and humanity of Christ, including both the Council of Nicaea (AD 325) and the Council of Chalcedon (AD 451).

The Christian tradition would come to identify first, Christ as the Creator of heaven and earth, visible and invisible. Defending the full divinity of Christ against Arius and with Athanasius, the Council of Nicaea affirmed Christ as Son of God, sharing in the same substance as the Father.[4] Likewise, this same passage also affirms Christ's humanity by describing him as "the image of the invisible God, the firstborn over all creation." The Council of Chalcedon affirmed Christ as fully human against those arguments made by Apollinarius, suggesting that Christ only "seemed" or "appeared" human rather than fully assuming flesh through the incarnation. Instead, the Council affirmed the union of two natures in the one person of Christ (known as the hypostatic union) in which Christ is described as both fully divine and fully human.[5]

Both Augustinian and Barthian theologies also affirm the full divinity and humanity of Christ. While cursory readings of Augustine dismiss his interest in Christology, Rowan Williams notes a "coherent Christological scheme" in Augustine's more mature writings such as *The Trinity* and *City of God*.[6] Additionally, scholars are turning to his *Expositions of the Psalms*,

---

[4] "The Creed of the Synod of Nicaea" (June 19, 325) in William G. Rusch, ed., *The Trinitarian Controversy* (Philadelphia: Fortress Press, 1980), 49.

[5] "Pope Leo I's Letter to Flavian of Constantinople," in Richard A. Norris Jr., ed., *The Christological Controversy* (Philadelphia: Fortress Press, 1980), 145–55.

[6] Rowan Williams, "Augustine's Christology: Its Spirituality and Rhetoric" in Peter W. Mathewes, ed., *In the Shadow of the Incarnation: Essays on Jesus Christ in the Early Church in Honor of Brian E. Daly* (Notre Dame: University of Notre Dame, 2008), 176.

sermons, and letters to discover an abundance of reflections on the centrality of Christ for understanding both God and the human person in Augustine's work.[7] Thus, in understanding Augustine's Christology, we set him in context with many of the Christological controversies circulating throughout the fourth and early fifth centuries.

In other words, Augustine's life and writing follow the Arian controversy over the divinity of Christ to which the Council of Nicaea responds in AD 325 and predate those arguments over the humanity of Christ culminating in the Council of Chalcedon in AD 451.[8] Overwhelmingly, Augustine's trinitarian and Christological writings both support the Nicene affirmations concerning the full divinity of Christ and perhaps anticipate the affirmation of the person of Christ that incorporates both divine and human natures codified at Chalcedon.

Likewise, Barth's own theology also affirms the full divinity and humanity of Christ in which Christ's coming to humanity in the form of the incarnation as Son of God is simultaneous to Christ's exaltation as Son of Man in his work of reconciliation.[9] As George Hunsinger describes it, this twofold reality involving Christ's divinity and humanity is beyond human comprehension, meriting dialectical description in which Barth describes only one side of the equation at a time.[10] Maintaining this tension, Barth affirms the councils of Nicaea and Chalcedon in their significance for understanding Christ as bringing together humanity and divinity in one person through the hypostatic union.

Thus, identifying the hypostatic union that affirms the full divinity and humanity of Christ in one person remains central to understanding whom persons image in relation to God. Interestingly, Paul uses the phrase "image of the invisible God" in Colossians 1 to describe Christ. For Paul, and subsequently Augustine and Barth, the image of God resides in the person of Christ, the new Adam who perfectly fulfills the law.[11] After the fall in Genesis 3, the image of God in humanity is dimmed or broken.

---

[7] Lewis Ayres, *Nicaea and Its Legacy* (Oxford: Oxford University Press, 2004).

[8] Brian Daly, "Christology" in Allan D. Fitzgerald, ed., *Augustine Through the Ages* (Grand Rapids: Eerdmans), 164.

[9] CD IV/1, 2.

[10] George Hunsinger, "Karl Barth's Christology," in John Webster, ed., *The Cambridge Companion to Karl Barth* (Cambridge: Cambridge University Press, 2000), 130.

[11] Col 1:17; Rom 5:12–21; Augustine, *The Trinity*; Barth, CD III/2 § 44.

Yet Paul affirms the true image in the person of Christ as bringing together the divine and human, eternal and temporal realms. Christ perfectly obeys the Father's will in union with God. Being fully God and fully human, the person of Christ embodies both what it means to be Creator and created. Given these dual natures, Christ comes to play the integral role in reconciliation between the Triune God and "all things" within creation. Because of this the Pauline tradition affirms that "He is before all things, and by Him all things hold together." Thus Paul initially establishes whom believers are called to image—that is, Christ, as they act and grow in union with the divine and human God-man. Moreover, Christ is the perfect image in his humanity as one in perfect fellowship with the Father through a posture of contemplation and action.

THE GOAL OF UNION WITH CHRIST: CONTEMPLATION AND ACTION
Walk in Him, rooted and built up in Him.

Action—"Walk in Him"

Now that Paul firmly establishes whom this Christ Jesus is that believers have received, the true image of God, he issues an imperative injunction that those same young believers "walk in Him" or act in him. The term "walk" evokes the image of movement or action as a body moving through space and time. The moral theologian could easily look at this passage and find this to be the most active verb or important theme within its context, moving listeners to act or live as imagers of Christ. Given my primary focus on two theologians, I interpret the meaning of moral action as most associated with love for Augustine and obedience for Karl Barth.

Augustine describes the moral life as one of love for both God and neighbor. Living in his historical time and context, Augustine borrowed from his Neoplatonist and Stoic philosophical influences that emphasized virtue as the key to happiness or the good life.[12] Like the Neoplatonists, Augustine came to understand evil as privation as opposed to the dualistic philosophy of Manichaeism as well as the importance of the eternal good or wisdom for

---

[12] James Wetzel, *Augustine and the Limits of Virtue* (Cambridge: Cambridge University Press, 1992), 1–16.

interpreting our temporal reality.[13] However, Augustine ultimately departs from Neoplatonism with its emphasis on the supremacy of reason for shaping the moral life and instead introduces the concept of the will as the locus in which one achieves or rejects virtue.[14]

Likewise, Augustine was influenced by the Stoics, particularly in their perception of the power of emotions to shape or skew reason in the pursuit of virtue. However, unlike the Stoics, Augustine comes to affirm the role of emotions as integral to the moral life, particularly in the role our affections play in determining our actions, revealing how our wills are ultimately directed at either love of God or love of self.[15] For Augustine, to walk or take moral action is to love in time—that is, primarily loving Christ in the neighbor.[16]

In addition, Paul's injunction to "walk" or "follow him" as moral action comes to be associated with obedience in the theology of Karl Barth. For Barth, morality is defined by God rather than humanity and is issued in the form of divine commands.[17] While morality takes the form of commands or injunctions from a divine lawgiver, Barth highlights how the commands are issued in the form of a covenant relationship between the Creator and humans. As Gerald McKenny describes it, the famous divine command is issued in the relational context of the covenant reality declaring, "I will be your God and you will be my people."[18]

However, not only does the God in Christ issue these commands, but the God in Christ also fulfills these commands. In this sense Christ is not only our justification before God but also our sanctification.[19] Christ fulfills the command of God as the perfect human who remains in steadfast communion with the Father that empowers his specific vocation or mission, including the Son's obedient descent in humility and his perfect obedience that results in human exaltation. Analogously, the key to the moral life or obedience resides in union with Christ, for Barth, the perfect harmony of the divine and human will that fulfills our human calling in time.

---

[13] Ibid.; Augustine, *Confessions*, trans. Henry Chadwick (Oxford: Oxford University Press, 1991); *The Trinity*, trans. Edmund Hill (Hyde Park, NY: New City Press, 1991).

[14] Wetzel, *Augustine and the Limits of Virtue*, 6–8, 45–55.

[15] Augustine, *City of God*.

[16] *City of God*, X; Eric Gregory, *Politics and the Order of Love* (Chicago: University of Chicago Press, 2008).

[17] CD II/2, III/4.

[18] Gerald McKenny, *The Analogy of Grace* (Cambridge: Cambridge University Press, 2010).

[19] CD II/2, 539.

Contemplation—"Rooted and Built Up in Him"

Understanding moral action leads to a second component regarding union with Christ. For Paul, in order to walk or act in Christ, one must be "rooted and built up in Him." So what does it mean to be rooted and built in him? For both Augustine and Barth, to walk or act morally from a disposition of union with Christ, one must cultivate inward communion or fellowship with Christ. For Augustine such union is primarily seen through contemplation in love of God, and for Barth such union is primarily understood through reception or response to the initiation of divine grace.[20]

For Augustine, to understand the meaning of union with Christ, one must first understand the meaning behind his famous "order of love." For Augustine love of God or love of self most defines the moral life. In *On Christian Teaching*, Augustine explains the order of love that ultimately defines our loves either in terms of love of God or love of self. Augustine claims that only one thing can be enjoyed for its own sake while all other goods (including self and neighbor) are to be "used" or loved for the sake of this ultimate good. For Augustine the one good that is to be truly enjoyed is the ultimate good, namely God.[21] Only God can be enjoyed or bring happiness to creatures, for only God is eternal. To place one's enjoyment or rest in a lower, created, or temporal good is to misuse that object in the form of a disordered love. Disordered love involves placing one's happiness in a temporary object rather than one's highest fulfillment in God.

Instead persons are to use lower goods or created goods in relation to ultimate love for God. It is easy to see how temporary goods such as food, sex, money, or prestige become disordered loves when individuals place their rest or enjoyment in these temporal goods. Such goods were not meant to satisfy in that they are only temporary rather than eternal. However, Augustine takes this meaning a step further and includes the neighbor, self, and loved ones. These goods, whether the distant neighbor or a close relationship, cannot satisfy humanity's ultimate need. Instead they become perverted desires when we love them for their own sake without reference to love of God. In many ways the order of love reflects Augustine's own understanding of the meaning of evil as privation or the absence of good. These created goods are not bad in

---

[20] Augustine, *The Trinity*; Barth, CD IV/2. See also Autumn Alcott Ridenour, "Union with Christ for the Aging: A Consideration of Aging and Death in the Theology of St. Augustine and Karl Barth," a dissertation submitted to Boston College, Lisa Sowle Cahill, director, September 2013.

[21] Augustine, *On Christian Teaching*, 9.

themselves but become distorted goods when we disorder our loves toward them through sin.

Not surprisingly, perhaps, such disordered love sounds much like idolatry in the first commandment's injunction not to have any graven image above God (Exod 20:3). Instead, we are called to love God with all our heart, soul, mind, and strength in order that we might love our neighbor as ourselves (Mark 12:30). But love must be ordered: first for God and then for neighbor and self. While perhaps sounding simple on the surface, the ordering of human loves and desires is actually a challenging one that pilgrims wrestle with throughout the duration of one's moral life before God.

Augustine's order of love aligns well with how Yale theologian Kathryn Tanner describes human creatures as "plastic" or "conformable material" since persons are made for molding or attaching themselves to someone or something.[22] Given that humans are made as "imagers" (bearing the *imago Dei*), we are made to image or attach ourselves to the ultimate source of our existence. However, since the fall and experience of sin, we know what it is to experience restlessness and attach ourselves to people or things that cannot ultimately satisfy. Our culture is replete with examples ranging from fashion to social networks to professional societies in which a general level of conformity occurs in every sphere of human existence. Humans are imitators by nature. We are pliable and conform to persons and goods around us. However, this conformity goes astray when it is not ordered to the ultimate source of our existence, the final good—that is, God in Jesus Christ, whom persons are ultimately called to love and image.

Interestingly, there is truth in an old adage that "you become what you love." The truth manifests itself as persons tend to order their lives around their greatest loves and desires. C. S. Lewis's depiction of the character Eustace from Narnia's *The Voyage of the Dawn Treader* portrays a selfish, whiny, arrogant English boy who eventually turns into a dragon for thinking "dragonish," self-centered thoughts.[23] In other words Eustace transforms into the dragonish thoughts that consume him. Eventually one's deepest affections and desires make themselves known through one's outward character or actions toward others. You are what you love. This is the meaning behind Augustine's famous order of love, a love eloquently portrayed in Lewis's *The Great Divorce*, in which persons are ultimately defined by love of God or love of self.[24]

---

[22] Kathryn Tanner, *Christ the Key* (Cambridge: Cambridge University Press, 2010).

[23] C. S. Lewis, *The Voyage of the Dawn Treader* (New York: Collier, 1986).

[24] C. S. Lewis, *The Great Divorce* (San Francisco: HarperCollins, 2001).

In a more recent interpretation of Augustine's *The Trinity*, both Rowan Williams and Lewis Ayres interpret Christ as the key to understanding Augustine's famous treatise on the triune God. In book XIII of *The Trinity*, Augustine comes to identify *sapientia* (wisdom) and *scientia* (knowledge) with Christ's divine and human natures.[25] *Sapientia* has to do with understanding eternal goods whereas *scientia* has to do with knowledge of the temporal realm (here including everything from the sciences to moral virtue). In Christ, Augustine proposes, the fullness of wisdom and knowledge comes together in that God's eternal or divine wisdom directs and corresponds with human knowledge, enacting perfect virtue or action in time.

Lewis Ayres finds the climax of *The Trinity* in Christ's person as the culmination of wisdom and knowledge that repairs the broken image of humanity.[26] In other words Augustine describes how Christ's person enacts virtue in time while maintaining union with the Father. Such union keeps Christ in tune to wisdom in a way that repairs the broken image of God in humanity. Rather than suffer the consequences of separated wisdom and knowledge as seen through the situation following the ill choice of Adam and Eve, instead, the union of wisdom and knowledge is renewed again in the person, work, and example of Christ.[27]

Later within *The Trinity*, Augustine describes wisdom and knowledge as analogous to the inner and outer person.[28] Wisdom is internal understanding while knowledge directs external action. In this sense wisdom and knowledge draw together the eternal and temporal, internal and external, or soul and bodily realities. Contemplation involves prayerful union with God while external moral action reflects this inward union with God to the broader world. Christ perfectly exhibits contemplation and action, prayer and activity through his own mission. Likewise, Christ calls persons to union with him as their deepest love through contemplation and action.

Not surprisingly, perhaps, Paul describes this same Christ, saying, "All the treasures of wisdom and knowledge are hidden in Him" (Col 2:3). In order to "walk" and "remain rooted and built up in Him" as Colossians 2:6–7 describes, persons must remain in union with the source of all wisdom and knowledge who brings the eternal wisdom and will of God together in human

---

[25] Augustine, *The Trinity*, XIII.6, 366–69.

[26] Lewis Ayres, "The Christological Context of Augustine's *De Trinitate* XIII: Toward Relocating Books VIII-XV," *Augustinian Studies* 29, no. 1 (1998): 111–39.

[27] Augustine, *The Trinity*, XII–XV.

[28] Augustine, *The Trinity*, XV.3, 407–13.

experience. In this way persons come more deeply to image God in union with Christ by bringing together wisdom and knowledge.

Likewise, Karl Barth writes of this same union in similar terms. Interestingly, one could read Barth's entire *Church Dogmatics* as God's movement toward humanity through the incarnation and our movement toward God through reconciliation.[29] Following the argument of Athanasius, Barth says God became human in order that we might "come to God."[30] For Barth, God eternally willed that we might fellowship with him. The reality of the hypostatic union brings together the divine and human realms in the person of Christ. Christ's person upheld union with God given he was both perfectly receptive to the Father through prayer while perfectly enacting his human mission or vocation in time.[31] This is seen throughout Christ's ministry and movement from Gethsemane to the cross. Prayer guided his moral action or mission.

Thus, much like Augustine's theology that brings contemplation and action together through the wisdom and knowledge of Christ, so too does Barth bring together the reception of divine grace with the response of moral action in time. For Barth imaging God in union with Christ means persons receive grace and respond with action in their historical and temporal realities. In this sense union with Christ is twofold, incorporating both wisdom and knowledge, contemplation and action as persons are both "rooted and built up in him" in the Pauline sense that "walks" or acts out of this relationship toward the neighbor through acts of love, mercy, and justice in time.

THE CHARACTERISTICS OF BEING REMADE IN THE IMAGE OF CHRIST

"Established in the faith, just as you were taught, overflowing with gratitude."

Third, union with Christ—through wisdom and knowledge, contemplation and action—leads to a sense of being renewed or remade in the image of Christ. Here I bring together Paul's final three characteristics of Colossians

---

[29] The Doctrine of revelation, election, creation, and reconciliation throughout *Church Dogmatics* inculcates Christ's twofold movement. Likewise, Adam Neder argues "participation" or "union with Christ" serves as the key to interpreting Barth's voluminous *Church Dogmatics* in Neder's *Participation in Christ* (Louisville, KY: Westminster John Knox Press, 2009).

[30] CD IV/2, 106.

[31] CD IV/2.

2:6–7 in which believers are called to be "established in the faith, just as you were taught, overflowing with gratitude."

For Augustine faith is precisely the link between eternal and temporal realities. Faith belongs to the realm of knowledge, or knowledge of the temporal realm, so that it might be ordered and enlightened by eternal wisdom.[32] Likewise, Thomas Aquinas claims faith resides in the intellect, transforming reason to guide the will that enacts the moral life.[33] Interestingly, the reformers Luther and Calvin place faith in the will rather than intellect, likening the role of faith to the term "trust" or "rest."[34] In this sense Thomas Aquinas interprets Augustinian faith by bringing together wisdom and knowledge while the Reformers interpret Augustinian (and Pauline) faith in terms of our deepest trust, rest, or love. Faith not only links temporal knowledge of the world as it exists here and now with eternal wisdom, but faith also reflects our greatest love or rest that both Paul and Augustine believe "comes to establish us." By establishing us, faith becomes our identity by which we rest and are known. In both senses of the term, faith plays an integral role for union with Christ that helps renew or remake our humanity in the image of God through Christ.

Next Paul emphasizes the role of teaching or imitating Christ. The established faith is one that is received and taught within the community of faith. Here again I emphasize Kathryn Tanner's description of human nature as one that naturally images or imitates what we see. Looking to children, we see how strong our capacity for imitation guides us, perhaps most clearly seen through the adoption of language but also through gestures and even attitudes children display. But the role of imitation or imaging exists not only for children but continues through adolescence, college, and into adulthood. Thus one must ask or consider what teachers or influences most persuade one's affections, thoughts, and will. This is not to claim believers should never study, sit, or learn from teachers or philosophies with different presuppositions or premises that challenge their own. In fact, Augustine appropriated what he found to be true in accordance with Christ from his philosophical and historical context and departed from these influences when he found

---

[32] Augustine, *The Trinity*, XIII.1, 3.

[33] St. Thomas Aquinas, *Summa Theologica*, I–II Q. 62 Art. 3 sed. Contra, trans by Fathers of the English Dominican Province (Notre Dame, IN: Ave Maria Press, 1981), 852–53.

[34] Martin Luther, "Freedom of a Christian," in John Dillenberger, ed., *Martin Luther: Selections from His Writings* (New York: Doubleday, 1962), 55–63; John T. McNeill, ed., *Calvin: Institutes of the Christian Religion*, III.2.29–36 (Louisville, KY: John Knox Press, 1960), 575–84.

these philosophies departed from his foundational understanding of Christ and the rule of faith for moral living. One only has to consider his appropriation of Neoplatonism in regard to the problem of evil and departure from Neoplatonism in regard to the value of the soul-body relation as an example.[35]

However, I am challenging believers to consider who serves as the ultimate teacher, the Holy Spirit, through union with Christ. Thus believers should have a discerning spirit that considers what teachers, colleagues, friends, and even media most influence their mind and affections and how these sources relate to faith. For Augustine and Barth, along with Pauline thought in Colossians, the role of the Holy Spirit serves as the ultimate teacher as believers remain in union with Christ. Every Christian will experience challenges to one's faith, entailing intellectual, emotional, and even physical challenges. However, the promise of Christ through Scripture is that believers will never be devoid of the presence of Christ, even in one's darkest hour (John 16:32–33).

The question will be whether believers continue, listening intently to Christ as the Good Shepherd, who leads, guides, and brings peace to life's difficult circumstances (John 10:27). This is where the good disciplines taught and practiced that regularly receiving Christ through Scripture, breaking bread, and fellowship within a community of faith continues to be of utmost importance for growth in moral spirituality. Involvement in the local church as a community of lived faith enacting the body of Christ is integral to the Christian moral life. The challenges facing faithful pilgrims journeying through this world reiterate the need to remain closely knit to Christ by maintaining close bonds of love with fellow members of the body through regular breaking of bread, preaching the word, and sharing life. In this way believers maintain a strong theological identity while culturally engaging their surrounding world.

Finally, the practice of established faith once taught and received through union with Christ that helps renew the image of God is daily reflected through a spirit of gratitude. Here Paul ends Colossians 2:7 by imploring believers to maintain a spirit that "overflows with gratitude." For Augustine gratitude is important for the believer, particularly in relation to a posture of humility as the response to God's love. A spirit of humility is perhaps a

---

[35] Augustine, *Confessions*; *City of God*.

foundational virtue for understanding one's core identity in terms of love of self or love of God.[36]

But for Karl Barth gratitude is the heart of the moral life. Gratitude is fundamental to following the Divine Command as an ethical agent in covenant relation with God.[37] In gratitude persons respond to God through obedience and a spirit of prayer that maintains union with Christ.[38] Gratitude and love are the reminders that one stands as a creature in union or covenant relation with God. By receiving and remaining in union with Christ, persons gratefully respond to this grace through obedience to God and service to others. As social psychologists more recently affirm, the great enemy of gratitude is pride or narcissism.[39] In many ways gratitude finds correlation with humility. Both draw one into the life of God and others.

In this sense gratitude is the appropriate response of a life lived in union with Christ. Gratitude brings together wisdom and knowledge, wisdom that reflects the eternal perspective that fills one's soul with joy or happiness as one lives and acts with knowledge or virtue in their surrounding world throughout the ebb and flow of life's circumstances. Gratitude helps maintain a receptive or contemplative posture toward God through receiving the grace and goodness associated with Christ while framing our outward actions, love, and service to others in our world. Thus, by Paul's three final attributes—faith, good teaching, and gratitude—believers help renew the image of God in their lives through union with Christ.

As Paul concludes in Colossians 3:9–10, this union helps believers to "put off the old self with its practices and . . . put on the new self. You are being renewed in knowledge according to the image of your Creator." Thus, putting on the new self entails union with the living God who helps believers grow in the knowledge and wisdom of Christ, the true image. By contemplation and action in Christ, receiving wisdom and knowledge in him, persons walk or morally act in ways that display Christ. This walk helps guard against what Paul calls "philosophy and empty deceit according to human tradition" that inevitably face pilgrims traveling through this world (Col 2:8). Nonetheless,

---

[36] "We see then that the two cities were created by two kinds of love: the earthly was created by self-love reaching the point of contempt of God, the Heavenly City by the love of God carried as far as contempt of self" in *City of God*, XIV.28, 593.

[37] CD III/4, 376.

[38] CD IV/2, 30.

[39] Robert A. Emmons and Charles M. Shelton, "Gratitude and the Science of Positive Psychology," in C. R. Snyder and Shane J. Lopez, eds., *Handbook of Positive Psychology* (Oxford: Oxford University Press, 2005), 459–60.

Paul admonishes persons to take heart, keep the faith, receive continued teaching, and maintain a posture of gratitude to help guard their spirits and deepest loves as they travel through time in union with both Christ and fellow believers. In this way believers enact the body of Christ through love and acts of service that bring the reality of Christ to their surrounding world.

CONCLUSION

Remaining in a strong vertical relation with the Divine, believers are empowered to live and enact virtue through horizontal relations with their neighbors. Believers contemplate or receive Christ in union with the Spirit that motivates them to enact virtues that serve their neighbors throughout time. In this sense both Augustine and Barth offer a strong sense of theological identity, propelling love of neighbor that includes convictional civility through cultural engagement. Strongly rooted in one's theological identity, one is free to receive, respond, and give to the neighbor—whether through dialogue, acts of service, or civic friendship.

Renewed in the image of Christ, believers are called to "put on heartfelt compassion, kindness, humility, gentleness, and patience, accepting and forgiving one another" (Col 3:12–13). Not only do they live more in harmony within the community of faith, but their theological identity should also empower their convictional civility with their surrounding world through a spirit of gratitude coupled with acts of love and service. Thus "established" in their theological identity through contemplation and action, the community of faith might more fully contribute to the common good or *civitas* within the broader world as pilgrims in union with Christ.

Baptists, Conscience, and Convictional Civility in Health Care

C. Ben Mitchell

Among many other good things, David S. Dockery is known for a pregnant term used to describe the ideal posture of a Christian in society: convictional civility. Convictional civility represents the mean of both virtues—conviction and civility—in a harmonious marriage. The excess or deficit of one or the other leads to discord. Civility without conviction tends toward sentimentalism or "niceness." Conviction without civility tends toward anarchy or tyranny, depending on who wields the power. I will argue that the marriage of these virtues is able to flourish best in a context where there is a free conscience and a free market. Where freedom of conscience is threatened and religious liberty is denied, civility may be at risk.

I maintain that convictional civility is thoroughly Christian, characteristically Baptist, and exceedingly consistent with the American context of a free church in a free society with a free market. Furthermore, I will argue that some of the current controversies we face in health care may be resolved by maintaining convictional civility in a free market.

A FREE CHURCH IN A FREE STATE

Where conviction may live without fear of government reprisal, civility may prevail. Where civility is threatened by coercive government, conviction must assert itself. This was certainly true in early American life. Roger Williams

(c. 1603–1683), the founder of Providence Plantation—which later became Rhode Island, was banished from the Massachusetts Bay Colony because he left the established church of the colony, believing instead that the sanctity of the human conscience demanded a free church in a free state, that civil government should afford the space for convictional belief and practice. In 1644, he published his desideratum, *The Bloudy Tenent of Persecution, for the Cause of Conscience, Discussed in a Conference Between Truth and Peace, Who, in All Tender Affection, Present to the High Court of Parliament, (as the Result of Their Discourse) These (Among Other Passages) of Highest Consideration*. In this manifesto he accused British Parliament, through its mandate of religious uniformity, of committing "a greater rape, then [sic] if they had forced or ravished the bodies of all the women in the *World*."[1] Although he may be accused of terse rhetoric, he was making a point he did not want to be misunderstood—that forcing a person through the power of the state to violate his or her own conscience was a monstrous harm, an incivility of the highest order.

Williams was not alone. Baptists in both England and America were vocal apologists for religious liberty and freedom of conscience for every person. According to one historian, "Baptists did not *turn* toward the idea of 'a free conscience.' They *began* in the seventeenth century screaming and agitating for liberty of conscience."[2] Because of coercive government restrictions, they suffered the pain of persecution in the jail cells, stockades, and whipping posts of Europe.

Thomas Helwys (c. 1575–1615), for instance, cofounded the first Baptist church on English soil in the early seventeenth century in Spitalfields, London. In 1612, he published *A Short Declaration of the Mystery of Iniquity*, arguing for liberty of conscience and forwarding a copy to King James I. In his inscription he wrote, "The king is a mortal man and not God, and therefore hath no power over the immortal souls of his subjects to make laws and ordinances for them and to set spiritual Lords over them."[3] Both Helwys and his

---

[1] Roger Williams, "The Bloudy Tenent of Persecution," in Daniel L. Dreisbach and Mark David Hall, eds., *The Sacred Rights of Conscience: Selected Readings on Religious Liberty and Church-State Relations in the American Founding* (Indianapolis: Liberty Fund, 2009), 151.

[2] Walter B. Shurden, "Baptist Freedom and the Turn Toward a Free Conscience: 1612/1652," in Michael E. Smith Sr. and Walter B. Shurden, eds., *Turning Points in Baptist History: A Festschrift in Honor of Harry Leon McBeth* (Atlanta: Mercer University Press, 2008), 22.

[3] Thomas Helwys, *The Life and Writings of Thomas Helwys*, ed. Joseph E. Early (Atlanta: Mercer University Press, 2009), 156.

wife, Joan, suffered for the cause of conscience, and Thomas died in Newgate Prison at the age of forty.

Like Roger Williams, Obadiah Holmes (1607–1682) was also banished from Massachusetts because of his Baptist beliefs, settling in Newport, Rhode Island. In 1651, Holmes and two friends, John Clarke and John Crandall, traveled back to Massachusetts to visit an aged and blind friend. After receiving Christian Communion in the friend's home, they were arrested for unlawful worship. They were convicted and sentenced to either a fine or whipping—a very uncivil punishment.[4]

Clarke and Crandall paid their fines or let friends pay them for them. Holmes, however, refused to pay, nor would he allow anyone to pay it on his behalf. He thus remained in prison. The law required that alternative to payment be exacted, namely, the guilty party was to be "well whipped." On September 6, 1651, Obadiah Holmes, a Baptist glassworker, was beaten with thirty stripes. As his clothes were being stripped from his back, Holmes declared, "I am now come to be baptized in afflictions by your hands, that so I may have further fellowship with my Lord. [I] am not ashamed of His sufferings, for by His stripes am I healed." One commentator says he was whipped "unmercifully." Yet following his beating, Holmes turned to the magistrates and said, "You have struck me with roses." Governor Jenks observed that "for many days, if not some weeks, he could take no rest but upon his knees and elbows, not being able to suffer any part of his body to touch the bed whereupon he lay."[5]

Speaking of his punishment later, Holmes testified:

> As the strokes fell upon me I had such a spiritual manifestation of God's presence as the like thereof I never had nor felt, nor can fleshly tongue express; and the outward pain was so removed from me that indeed I am not able to declare it, yea, and in a manner felt it not, although it was grievous, as the spectators said, the man striking with all his strength (yea, spitting in his hand three times, as many affirmed) with a three-corded whip, giving me therewith thirty strokes.[6]

---

4   See Obadiah Holmes's "Last Will and Testimony," December 20, 1675, in Edwin S. Gaustad, ed., *Baptist Piety: The Last Will and Testimony of Obadiah Holmes* (Grand Rapids: Christian University Press, 1978), 73.

5   Ibid., 29.

6   Cited in William Cathcart, *Baptist Encyclopaedia* (Philadelphia: L. H. Everts, 1881), 539.

Because early Baptists were preachers before they were professors, much of what they had to say about liberty of conscience was couched in sermons instead of research papers. But these were sermons unlike what most of us have ever heard in our lifetimes. For instance, John Leland (1754–1841) was a Baptist minister in both Massachusetts and Virginia. He preached in Orange County, Virginia, from the nation's founding in 1776 to1791. During that time he became friends with James Madison, Thomas Jefferson, and other American founders. Part of a campaign promise Madison made to Leland and several other Baptists led to the adoption of the Bill of Rights as amendments to the Constitution, especially the free exercise clause of the First Amendment: "Congress shall make no law respecting an establishment of religion, or prohibiting the free exercise thereof; or abridging the freedom of speech, or of the press; or the right of the people peaceably to assemble, and to petition the Government for a redress of grievances." In a sermon preached in 1791, Leland declared:

> The word conscience signifies common science, a court of judicature which the Almighty has erected in every human breast; a *censor morum* [moral judge] over all his actions. Conscience will ever judge right when it is rightly informed, and speak the truth when it understands it. But to advert to the question—"Does a man upon entering into social compact surrender his conscience to that society to be controlled by the laws thereof, or can he in justice assist in making laws to bind his children's consciences before they are born?" I judge not, for the following reasons:
>
> 1. Every man must give an account of himself to God, and therefore every man ought to be at liberty to serve God in that way that he can best reconcile it to his conscience. If government can answer for individuals at the day of judgment, let men be controlled by it in religious matters; otherwise let men be free.
>
> 2. It would be sinful for a man to surrender that to man which is to be kept sacred for God. A man's mind should be always open to conviction, and an honest man will receive that doctrine which appears the best demonstrated; and what is more common than for the best of men to change their minds? Such are the prejudices of the mind, and such the force of tradition, that a man who never alters his mind is either very weak or very stubborn. How painful then must it be to

an honest heart to be bound to observe the principles of his former belief after he is convinced of their imbecility? and this ever has and ever will be the case while the rights of conscience are considered alienable.

3. But supposing it was right for a man to bind his own conscience, yet surely it is very iniquitous to bind the consciences of his children; to make fetters for them before they are born is very cruel. And yet such has been the conduct of men in almost all ages that their children have been bound to believe and worship as their fathers did, or suffer shame, loss, and sometimes life; and at best to be called dissenters, because they dissent from that which they never joined voluntarily. Such conduct in parents is worse than that of the father of Hannibal, who imposed an oath upon his son while a child never to be at peace with the Romans.

4. Finally, religion is a matter between God and individuals, religious opinions of men not being the objects of civil government nor any ways under its control.[7]

For Leland the social compact, membership in a civil society, does not proscribe the exercise of conscience precisely because government must not attempt to control the conscience in a civil society.

Another slightly more recent example comes from the famous Texas Baptist, George W. Truett (1867–1944). Truett was pastor of First Baptist Church, Dallas, from 1897 until his death in 1944. In the shadow of World War I, on Sunday, May 16, 1920, during the annual meeting of the Southern Baptist Convention held in Washington, D.C., Truett spoke from the steps of the Capitol to 10,000–15,000 people. J. B. Gambrell, then president of the Southern Baptist Convention, said of Truett's sermon, "Since Paul spoke before Nero, no Baptist speaker ever pleaded the cause of truth in surroundings so dignified, impressive and inspiring."

What did Truett say with such prophetic boldness? "[I]n the shadow of our country's Capitol, compassed about as we are with so great a cloud of witnesses, let us today renew our pledge to God, and to one another, that we

---

[7] John Leland, "The Rights of Conscience Inalienable" in Ellis Sandoz, ed., *Political Sermons of the American Founding Era, 1730–1805*, vol. 2 (Indianapolis: Liberty Fund, 1998), 1,085–86.

will give our best to church and to state, to God and to humanity, by his grace and power, until we fall on the last sleep."[8]

For Truett the "best" Baptists could give to their country was to work tirelessly to preserve the best context for the expression of convictional civility.

> Indeed, the supreme contribution of the new world to the old is the contribution of religious liberty. This is the chiefest contribution that America has thus far made to civilization. And historic justice compels me to say that it was pre-eminently a Baptist contribution. The impartial historian, whether in the past, present or future, will ever agree with our American historian, Mr. Bancroft, when he says: "Freedom of conscience, unlimited freedom of mind, was from the first the trophy of the Baptists." And such historian will concur with the noble John Locke who said: "The Baptists were the first propounders of absolute liberty, just and true liberty, equal and im-partial liberty." Ringing testimonies like these might be multiplied indefinitely.[9]

These texts remind us that, on the one hand, what professors Daniel Dreisbach and Mark David Hall have called "the sacred rights of conscience,"[10] were secured at a tremendous price. On the other hand they remind us that, as Truett said, although it was largely a Baptist contribution, it was for the common good. So, although the protection of liberty of conscience may have been an achievement of a particular religious group during a particular mo-ment in history, its benefits accrued then, and now, to everyone. Human con-science offers the expression of conviction that a civil society accommodates, and even invites, from her membership.

Although conflicts of conscience are episodic and relatively limited, they are becoming increasingly frequent as our society becomes more pluralistic. For instance, several years ago in Minneapolis, Minnesota, approximately two-thirds of taxi drivers were Muslims from Somalia. Some clerics main-tain that the Koran's prohibition against *consuming* alcohol extends to *trans-porting* alcohol. Thus, some Muslim cab drivers at the Minneapolis airport

---

[8]   George W. Truett, "Baptists and Religious Liberty," in *A Texas Baptist History Sourcebook: A Companion to McBeth's Texas Baptists,* ed. Joseph E. Early Jr. (Denton, TX: University of North Texas Press, 2004), 179.

[9]   Ibid., 166.

[10] Daniel L. Dreisbach and Mark David Hall, eds., *The Sacred Rights of Conscience: Selected Readings on Religious Liberty and Church-State Relations in the American Founding* (India-napolis: Liberty Fund, 2009).

refused to transport passengers visibly carrying alcohol from the duty-free airport stores. This was presumably based on religious conscience.[11]

In April 2007, the Minnesota Airports Commissioners unanimously decided that a taxi driver must transport passengers carrying alcohol or face a thirty-day suspension. A subsequent refusal would result in a two-year suspension. The Minnesota Court of Appeals heard the case and, in September 2008, ratified a lower court's ruling on the grounds that the drivers did not suffer irreparable harm. Is this really the best we can do? Does this decision reflect the wedding of the virtues of conviction and civility? Must every appeal to conscience result in endless trials? As one commentator said, this seems like an "unenlightened, unimaginative resolution of the dispute."[12]

CONVICTIONAL CIVILITY AND A FREE MARKET IN HEALTH CARE

Recent controversies in health care challenge us to cultivate the space for convictional civility. For instance, health-care workers' rights of conscience continue to be hotly debated. In a civil society, may doctors and nurses refuse to practice abortions or distribute abortifacient drugs without fear of legal penalties? University of Chicago physician-ethicist Farr Curlin and his colleagues point out that, historically, doctors and nurses have not been required to participate in procedures that violated their consciences, e.g., to participate in abortions or assist in suicides.[13] In fact, legislation in states where those practices are legal have, more often than not, included conscience clauses to protect health-care professionals. Ironically, in some cases those protocols require physicians to refer patients to another doctor who will perform a procedure they find unconscionable (perhaps better characterized as a conscience clause without a conscience!).

More recently controversies over emergency contraceptives have led some to criticize the existence of these conscience clauses. For instance, Alta Charo, the outspoken professor of law and bioethics at the University of Wisconsin at Madison, "suggests that the conflict about conscience clauses

---

[11] Stephanie Simon, "Where Faith and Work Collide," *Los Angeles Times*, March 27, 2007, A10, accessed May 28, 2014, http://articles.latimes.com/2007/mar/27/nation/na-somali27.
[12] Cited in Thomas A. Cavanaugh, "Professional Conscientious Objection in Medicine with Attention to Referral," *Ave Maria Law Review* 9, no. 1 (2010).
[13] Farr A. Curlin, M.D., Ryan E. Lawrence, M.Div., Marshall H. Chin, M.D., M.P.H., and John Lantos, M.D., "Religion, Conscience, and Controversial Clinical Practices," *New England Journal of Medicine* 356, no. 6 (February 8, 2007): 594.

'represents the latest struggle with regard to religion in America,' and she criti-
cizes those medical professionals who would claim an 'unfettered right to personal autonomy while holding monopolistic control over a public good.'"[14]
Even more stridently Oxford ethicist Julian Savulescu has ranted: "A doctor's
conscience has little place in the delivery of modern medical care . . . if people
are not prepared to offer legally permitted, efficient, and beneficial care to a
patient because it conflicts with their values, they should not be doctors."[15]
So, apparently, conviction may only be one-sided when it comes to physicians
and the law. What about the convictions of those who refuse to perform abortions for the sake of their conscience?

What Curlin, et al., demonstrate empirically is that physicians themselves
are divided about the role of conscience in clinical practice. In their study
of more than 1,000 physicians (n=1,144), they found that most physicians
believe it is ethically permissible for doctors to explain their moral objections
to patients. Sixty-three percent thought explaining their moral objections to
certain procedures was not a violation of the physician-patient relationship.
Eighty-six percent believed doctors are obligated to present all options to
patients, even those the doctor thinks are morally dubious; and 71 percent
thought they should refer a patient to another clinician who does not object
to the procedure. Furthermore, 52 percent reported objections to abortion
for failed contraception, and 42 percent objected to prescribing contraception for adolescents without parental consent.

Curlin and colleagues suggest that conflict about the role of conscience
in health care might be understood "in the context of perennial debates about
medical paternalism and patient autonomy."[16] They rightly worry that, if
their results are accurate, in many cases a patient's right to informed consent
is jeopardized by a physician's refusal to provide information about medical
procedures they themselves find problematic but are nonetheless consistent
with contemporary standards of care. "If physicians' ideas translate into their
practices," they say,

> then 14% of patients—more than 40 million Americans—may be
> cared for by physicians who do not believe they are obligated to dis-
> close information about medically available treatments they consider
> objectionable. In addition, 29% of patients—or nearly 100 million

---

[14] Ibid.
[15] Ibid.
[16] Ibid., 597.

Americans—may be cared for by physicians who do not believe they have an obligation to refer the patient to another provider for such treatments.[17]

It is becoming increasingly important, then, that we understand what we are claiming when we claim protection of freedom of conscience.

What do we say, for instance, when under invocation of conscience:

- a lab tech refuses to dispose of frozen embryos at a fertility clinic?
- a cardiologist refuses to deprogram a dying patient's ICD or pacemaker?
- a respiratory tech refuses to turn off a ventilator?
- a physician refuses to prescribe Viagra to a widower?
- an administrator refuses to approve funds for research she finds morally objectionable?
- under a regime of legalized assisted suicide, a physician in Oregon, Washington, or Montana refuses to prescribe a lethal overdose requested by a patient?

H. Tristram Engelhardt Jr. has famously argued that we live in a society of moral strangers who lack a shared, content-*full*, morality.[18] In his view the best we can do in a pluralist society is to agree to function with a secular, minimalist morality. Whether or not the situation is as dire as he suggests, Engelhardt is obviously correct in pointing out that we live in a pluralistic culture. When it comes to life, health, illness, disease, aging, disability, death, and many other existential aspects of our experience as human beings, we have diverse beliefs, values, and concerns. This complex set of beliefs, values, and concerns both shape and reflect our individual consciences.

Generally speaking, conscience may either function judicially or legislatively. Our judicial conscience is that faculty of our moral psychology that may evoke guilt when we do something we believe to be wrong, as when we speak of "pangs of conscience." But conscience may also be legislative when it informs our decision-making prior to acting. So we sometimes say, "Let conscience be your guide" when making decisions. My guess is that our legislative consciences would lead some of us to different answers to the questions above than others of us.

However diverse our convictions may be, we need a distinction between idiosyncratic—or what I might call solipsistic conscience—and other

---

[17] Ibid.
[18] H. Tristram Engelhardt Jr., *The Foundations of Bioethics*, 2nd ed. (New York: Oxford University Press, 1996), *passim*.

conceptions of conscience. University of Saint Thomas School of Law professor Robert Vischer convincingly argues that with respect to the protections
of the state, conscience is not a lone, renegade "black box," as though when
someone says, "My conscience tells me thus or so," we cannot inquire further.
Conscience claims should not serve as a political trump card. When someone
invokes "conscience" as a reason for either acting or refusing to act, we must
distinguish between one's individual, atomistic, idiosyncratic reasons and a
genuine appeal to conscience, says Vischer. In other words, there is a difference between individual preferences and conscience. "Conscience," he argues,
"should not be used as legal shorthand for an individual's liberty from government coercion on matters pertaining to her core moral convictions. The cause
of conscience encompasses individual liberty from state coercion, to be sure,
but it should not be defined solely as such."[19]

Conscience, Vischer maintains, corresponds to our social nature, and is
not merely an expression of our personal identity:

> Its [conscience's] claims are formed, articulated, and lived out along
> paths that transcend the individual. The vibrancy of conscience thus
> depends on more than the law's protection of individual autonomy;
> it also depends on the vitality of associations . . . against which the
> right of conscience is currently being invoked. Put simply, if our so-
> ciety is to facilitate an authentic and robust liberty of conscience, it
> cannot reflexively favor individual autonomy against group author-
> ity; it must also work to cultivate spaces in which individuals come
> together to live out the shared dictates of conscience.[20]

He also claims that,

> conscience, by its very nature, directs our gaze outward, to sources of
> formation, to communities of discernment, and to venues for expres-
> sion. When the state closes down avenues by which persons live out
> their core beliefs—and admittedly, some avenues must be closed if
> peaceful coexistence is to be possible—there is a cost to the contin-
> ued vitality of conscience.[21]

One important example he provides is the Civil Rights Act of 1964, which
prohibits discrimination based on race by employers and places of public

---

[19] Robert K. Vischer, *Conscience and the Common Good: Reclaiming the Space Between Person
and State* (Cambridge, England: Cambridge University Press, 2010), 36.
[20] Ibid., 6.
[21] Ibid., 4.

accommodation, including restaurants, schools, and hotels. Some readers are old enough to remember the social turmoil, especially in the South, over the legislation. Essentially, the government imposed "a collective vision of racial equality on public and private actors alike."[22] Despite any individual's or any group's appeal to conscience, the state mandated compliance with the law.

Here Vischer makes an interesting observation. Though he agrees it was necessary in this case, he wonders whether the Civil Rights Act "short-circuited the 'bottom-up' conversation"[23] over the common good by imposing a top-down solution, enshrining one set of claims as binding law and effectively shutting down the moral marketplace. In other words, because the virtue of civility had been eroded in the public square, personal convictions had to be coerced. Again, ultimately, he says, enforcement of the Civil Rights Act was the right thing to do. But lawmakers must carefully calculate the costs of making such decisions.

> The point is that figuring out how best to protect conscience without jeopardizing the common good, the law must pay attention to the substance of conscience's claims and to their impact on the state's legitimate pursuit of the common good. . . . The basis and content of conscience's claims matter, not because they provide bright-line boundaries of legitimacy, but because protecting conscience in a pluralistic democracy is a messy business, requiring ongoing conversations that are nuanced, widely engaged, and substantive. These may be obvious points with which few will disagree (I hope), but our legislatures and courts must work to identify and articulate more carefully the relationship between a proposed state incursion on conscience and the common good.[24]

To complicate matters, as Dan Sulmasy, professor of medicine and ethics in the Department of Medicine and the Divinity School at the University of Chicago, has opined, health-care institutions are also moral agents.[25] That is, health-care institutions—like hospitals, nursing homes, pharmacies, and the like—are more than mere aggregates of persons. They are, Sulmasy says, organizations with identifiable purposes and identity. "Almost all have explicit mission statements. They act intentionally. They make decisions for which

---

[22] Ibid., 27.

[23] Ibid.

[24] Ibid., 30.

[25] Daniel P. Sulmasy, "What Is Conscience and Why Is Respect for It So Important?," *Theoretical Medical Bioethics* 29 (2008): 143.

they may receive praise or blame. They have recognized institutional structures by which the decisions of some (e.g., the Board of Trustees, the CEO,
the Dean of the School of Nursing, or the Chair of Medicine) count as the
decisions of the institution."[26] And if health-care institutions are moral agents,
they too must be understood to have consciences. So institutional conscience,
with its fundamental commitment to act consistently with its conception of
morality, must also be respected by the law. Messy business made yet messier.

This is not how things worked in Chicago under former Illinois governor
Rod Blagojevich. In 2005, the governor ordered all pharmacies serving the
public to dispense "all FDA-approved drugs or devices that prevent pregnan-
cy . . . without delay, consistent with the normal timeframe for filling any
other prescription."[27] In Blagojevich's words, "Filling prescriptions for birth
control is about protecting a woman's right to have access to the medicine
her doctor says she needs. Nothing more. Nothing less. We will vigorously
protect that right."[28] Never mind the rights of conscience of pharmacists or
the pharmacy as a moral agent. "Efforts by pharmacy chains to carve out their
own policies on the issue were immediately squelched," observes Vischer.[29]

Draconian policies often result in other harms. For instance, I recently
learned of a practice apparently common in at least one region of the country.
It is the pharmacy analogue to the "slow code" in a hospital. In a slow code,
even though hospital policy may require that when a code is announced on
the loudspeaker, signaling that a patient is having a heart event, all personnel
in the area are to respond to the patient in trouble, everyone knows that if
doctors, nurses, and others do not think the patient should be resuscitated,
they move slowly toward the patient's bedside; hence, a *slow* code. Similarly,
when some pharmacists receive calls asking if they have emergency contraceptives they find morally problematic, they ask the caller to hold a moment; they
put down the phone, pick it up after the appropriate lapse of time, and say:
"No, I'm sorry, we're out of that." Of course, they had the drugs in stock, but
they gamed the system, deceived the client—and, I would argue, potential-
ly harmed their own souls by instituting a practice of lying—albeit, in order

---

[26] Ibid.

[27] "Governor Blagojevich Moves to Make Emergency Contraceptives Rule Permanent," State
of Illinois, Department of Financial and Professional Regulation, Official Press Release, April
18, 2005.

[28] Ibid.

[29] Robert K. Vischer, "Individual Rights vs. Institutional Identity: The Relational Dimension
of Conscience in Health Care," *Ave Maria Law Review* 9 (2010–2011): 70–71.

not to commit what they think is a greater evil. Although I may personally applaud their ingenuity, I think it's a bad practice to formalize. Bad policies that leave no room for conscientious objections encourage professionals to become mendacious.

CONCLUSION

Vischer would say in this case that "pitting one form of individual liberty against another form of individual liberty ignores the institutional liberty that is essential for the long-term flourishing of conscience."[30] An appeal to conscience is used to justify legislation that might enable pharmacists to refuse to fill prescriptions that violate their moral judgments. Similarly, conscience is invoked to justify legislation that would enable individuals to compel pharmacists to fill any legally obtained prescription. This is an irresolvable impasse.

Instead, for the sake of the common good, we should appeal to the moral marketplace for remedy. In other words, in a free-market democracy we should allow pharmacies (and hospitals) the opportunity to build moral claims into their corporate identities and let the market sort it out. Pharmacists will then be able to integrate their personal beliefs with their professional calling. In other words, they will be able to exercise convictional civility. Except in rare situations, patients will be able to access the drugs or procedures they want. Pharmacies would be required only to make their policies known to prospective patients (in the same way some states require restaurants to post nutritional values).

Where genuine access problems exist, the state might be justified in instantiating other remedies. But these will be the exception rather than the rule. "If we value a society with morally distinct institutions," says Vischer, "we must discern between market-driven inconvenience and market-driven lack of access. The latter warrants state intervention; the former does not."[31]

In a lovely expression Vischer states, "Rather than making all pharmacies morally fungible via state edict, the market allows the flourishing of plural moral norms in the provision of pharmaceuticals."[32] Furthermore, and as importantly, the sanctity of conscience would be protected. No one would be forced to fill prescriptions they find morally repugnant or feel they are morally complicit in evil.

---

[30] Ibid., 73.
[31] Vischer, *Conscience and the Common Good*, 173.
[32] Ibid., 156.

If this scheme, or something like it, turns out to be the case, pharmacists will be able to follow their convictions without violating civil law. If, by law, pharmacists are forced to violate their consciences or resign from the profession, we will have lost a huge health-care and cultural resource. Worse, we will have lost the soul of civility. Maintaining the balance between conviction and civility is not easy. But violating the one for the sake of the other creates perilous hardships.

Afterword

Gregory Alan Thornbury

In Judaism an apprentice aspires to be like his rabbi. This apprentice, or *talmid*, sticks close to his teacher, so much so that it is said of the student, "May I walk in the dust of the rabbi." As Matthew 10:24 explains to us, this is more than enough work for a lifetime. And yet the truth of the matter is that any great teacher realizes the goal of education is intergenerational. As Immanuel Kant observed in his lectures *On Pedagogy*, "One generation cannot work out a complete plan of education."[1] So all the while a student is trying to imitate the master, the teacher sees himself creating a project he could never possibly finish. To do this, he must invest himself not only in ideas and projects but also in people.

For the past twenty years it has been my privilege to count myself an apprentice of David Samuel Dockery. He is a man who understands his job is to carry on the work of giants of the faith and worthy forbears. Consider the following example: we should aspire to be like Paul Reid, the sixty-three-year-old sometime journalist for the *Palm Beach Post* who became William Manchester's unlikely choice to finish the third volume of his magisterial biography of Winston Churchill: *The Last Lion*.[2] None of us are up to the

---

[1] Immanuel Kant, as cited in Ellwood Patterson Cubberley, *Readings in the History of Education* (New York: Houghton Mifflin, 1920), 537.

[2] See James Andrew Miller, "A Problem of Churchillian Proportions," in the *New York Times*, November 1, 2012, accessed July 7, 2014, http://www.nytimes.com/2012/11/04/magazine/the-fan-who-finished-william-manchesters-churchill-biography.html?pagewanted=all&_r=0.

task of representing the kingdom of God in our time when we compare ourselves to the worthies who have gone before us. David Dockery looks to the great theologians of the past and understands that, while we cannot reprise their genius, we can be faithful to the great Christian intellectual tradition of which we take part.

I met David Dockery when he was vice president for academic administration and dean of the School of Theology at Southern Seminary when I first arrived at that place in 1993. I was accepted at the seminary even before R. Albert Mohler was appointed the president there in the spring of that year. I bring that up because I remember wondering what my seminary life would be like. My godly father, who pastored the same congregation in central Pennsylvania for forty-three years, reassured me: "David Dockery is there, and he's an evangelical, and he's the dean. He'll bring good people there to teach." Father knows best.

When I took David Dockery's class in systematic theology, I felt like I put on my regal robes studying the venerable dead with David Dockery. I had never heard anyone lecture on the seven ecumenical councils with such passion and verve. As I have written elsewhere, the great theologian Carl F. H. Henry helped save my faith in college, but David Dockery made me want to become a theologian. After I had completed the theology sequence with him, he invited me to become his grading fellow when he taught the course again. In that role I saw the seminary's tradition of gentleman scholar on display *par excellence*. I wanted to become a part of that legacy.

When he gave me the opportunity to candidate for a position as a philosophy professor at Union University, it changed my life forever. It set me on a course in Christian higher education. And when I walk into my office at The King's College on 56 Broadway in Manhattan, I often think about the fact that none of this would have been possible without David Dockery's personal investment in me. When I was a professor, he taught me how to engage students in the classroom. When I became a dean, he showed me how to balance the realities of administrative priorities with faculty concerns. When I was given an opportunity to serve in senior leadership at the university, he modeled wisdom behind the scenes that is the stuff of legend, but more important was the day-in, day-out heroism that took a small regional Baptist institution and turned it into a nationally respected university. We are in his debt.

This volume is filled with reflections on Dockerian themes. As one of his disciples, I have the honor of giving the last word. And here are the following lessons we are still learning from him.

WE ARE CALLED TO BE LEGATEES

One of the most remarkable (and might I add unrepeatable?) aspects of the Dockery legacy is his astonishing scholarly written output produced in the midst of a remarkable institutional turnaround. Among the most important of these were a number of key works, such as *Renewing Minds* and *The Great Tradition of Christian Thinking*, which addressed the nature, future of, and prospectus for Christian higher education.[3] These books have a persistent refrain to the great Christian intellectual tradition. Like his mentor James Leo Garrett, Dockery will impress you with his mastery of church history and where theologians have stood on every imaginable subject throughout the ages.

In Dockery's worldview the greatest tyranny is that which is novel. For him orthodoxy is always relevant. But in order to do this, we must listen to, lean in, and read closely the theologians and great Christian writers who have gone before us and framed our experience as believers. This is the central burden of our time. As the German philosopher Rüdiger Safranksi, biographer of both Nietzsche and Heidegger, has defined hermeneutics: it is the responsibility to listen, to not be more stupid than you already are. It is a refusal to gamble away your potential. Dockery comes by this conviction naturally: it was the principal focus of his graduate research. In his seminal work, *Biblical Interpretation Then and Now: Contemporary Hermeneutics in the Light of the Early Church*, he sets forth this standard: understand the church fathers and you will be prepared to weather the slings and arrows of outrageous postmodern fortune.[4]

The entire Dockery corpus, both written and institutional, has a rhetorical arc. You will never be greater than your familiarity with your Christian literary and theological heroes. As he explains in *Renewing Minds*, we want to do more than just train pious men and women in our colleges and

---

[3] David S. Dockery, *Renewing Minds: Serving Church and Society Through Christ-Centered Education* (Nashville: B&H, 2008); with Timothy George, *The Great Tradition of Christian Thinking: A Student's Guide* (Wheaton, IL: Crossway, 2012); *Faith and Learning: A Handbook for Christian Higher Education* (Nashville: B&H, 2012).

[4] David S. Dockery, *Biblical Interpretation Then and Now: Contemporary Hermeneutics in the Light of the Early Church* (Grand Rapids: Baker Academic, 2000).

universities. In the words of T. S. Eliot, we want them to learn "how to think in Christian categories."[5] According to Dockery, there is no way to cultivate such a program without fostering a theology of gratefulness and receipt for the prophets, apostles, martyrs, fathers, and saints of old. I vividly remember all of those convocation addresses at Union University, sitting next to my colleagues in full regalia, listening to him carefully explaining how Clement of Alexandria, a layman, helped shape the Christian mind in the West. The message: you don't need to be a professional theologian to integrate theology with your discipline. We often say we stand on the shoulders of giants. Dockery showed us how.

WE ARE CALLED TO DEFEND INSTITUTIONS

In a recent edition of *Comment* magazine, philosopher and editor James K. A. Smith observed the strange death wish young evangelicals have for their long-standing institutions:

> In a cynical age that tends to glorify "start-ups" and celebrate anti-institutional suspicion, faith in institutions will sound dated, stodgy, old-fashioned, even (gasp) "conservative." So Christians who are eager to be progressive, hip, relevant, and creative tend to buy into such anti-institutionalism, thus mirroring and mimicking wider cultural trends (which, ironically, are parasitic upon institutions!).[6]

Smith draws attention to an all too familiar problem in today's Christian culture: too many critics/armchair quarterbacks, and not enough humble and self-sacrificing leaders. For people like me, the remarkable success of Union University during the time of Dockery's tenure in that place, which began in 1996, set the stage for hope that evangelical institutions could flourish even in difficult days. What made him different, however, was that the institution was not *sui generis*; it always bore reference to something greater. At Union he wanted to represent Southern Baptists and evangelicalism well. As chairman of the board of the CCCU, it was Christ-centered higher education. With the Manhattan Declaration, it is religious liberty and the Great Tradition. He is always pointing us higher.

---

[5] Dockery, *Renewing Minds*, 11. Dockery quotes T. S. Eliot, *Christianity and Culture* (New York: Mariner, 1960), 22.

[6] James K. A. Smith, "We Believe in Institutions," *Comment* (Fall 2013): 2.

Institutions are the principal means by which we bear witness to the king-dom of God in our time. Everywhere one looks, evangelical institutions are in crisis. Many live one breath, even one pay period, from disaster. Meanwhile our credibility suffers. Good people lose jobs. The commonwealth is weak-ened. But by building institutions, you not only defend them. It's a defense of the faith, once removed.

Institution building takes more than lofty ideas and grandiose state-ments. Every institution can do that; it's called inflation. I remember talking to Os Guinness years ago about this. No one, he said, will ever be fooled that one of our institutions competes with the Ivy Leagues. They're several centu-ries ahead in terms of a head start. But what we can do is talk about vocation and put policies, systems, and procedures in place that can help people pursue their callings from God. In so doing we become facilitators of meaning in the world for Christ, and this is not just for colleges and universities but for schools, churches, denominations, businesses, and nonprofits. Says Smith: "If you're really passionate about fostering the common good, then you should resist anti-institutionalism. Because institutions are ways to love our neigh-bours. Institutions are durable, concrete structures that—when functioning well—cultivate all of creation's potential towards what God desires: *shalom*, peace, goodness, justice, flourishing, delight."[7]

Such a realization does not mean, however, that we do not aspire to the same metrics and data performance of great institutions that inspire us. One of the things that set the project of Union University under David Dockery's leadership apart was that he led the institution through carefully planned, board-approved, and systematically executed strategic plans. These docu-ments, written with both qualitative and quantitative goals in mind, required everyone in leadership to become, in essence, a data nerd. Unless you clear-ly decide where you want to be and unless you write your goals, you will at best be accidentally touring toward institutional excellence. In the early days David Dockery heavily shaped the language of Union's strategic plans. Over time his team took the lead, and his expertise entered toward the end of the process. In this way institutional strength matured from being primarily lead-er centered to team centered over a period of time.

Sadly we live in an age in which poor planning and loss of confidence in our evangelical institutions spell trouble for some organizations on the brink. In the years to come, some will close their doors. There will also be roll-up;

---

[7] Ibid.

institutions will merge boards and resources to stay alive. But what is need-ed immediately is the long view that Dockery brought to a place like Union in 1996 and that he will no doubt bring to other institutions again in the days to come.

WE ARE CALLED TO CHANGE THE TONE

When Carla Sanderson, C. Ben Mitchell, and I first discussed doing this *Festschrift*, we debated what the right title would be to summarize Dockery's ongoing legacy. We talked about scholarship and theological conviction, a tandem that defines his life and career. We talked about excellence in leader-ship, which he has brought to the many institutions he has served throughout his career. But one phrase David Dockery has used about the voice of the Christian community in these days of opportunity and challenge kept ringing in my ears: *convictional civility*. It's a phrase I hear others using now, but David Dockery was the first one I ever heard employ the phrase. This volume has considered this theme from a number of perspectives.

But for me the spirit of this phrase was captured at a moment in time. In 1962, five American theologians were invited to have a dialogue with Karl Barth at the University of Chicago Divinity School. American evangelicals, of course, had serious questions about the German theologian's understand-ing of divine revelation and doctrine of salvation. One of the five to meet with Barth was then-Fuller Seminary president, E. J. Carnell. When Carnell returned from his meeting with Barth to speak to Fuller faculty and stu-dents about the encounter, what they were expecting was no doubt the tale of a great debate. In this Carnell disappointed them somewhat. Although he would speak of their differences later in his talk, he threw cold water on con-troversy. Carnell described the thoughtful and kind way Barth had engaged in the dialogue. In sum he thought Barth was Christlike. Jesus came as the only Son from the Father, he remarked, full of grace and truth. To this Carnell, in an authoritative voice, added to the seminary students whom he led: "Never get the order wrong."

David Dockery's leadership is characterized by grace and truth. And time after time, he has endeavored not to get the order wrong. Some time ago I was conversing with an SBC colleague about the prospects of doing this book. This particular (young) pastor and scholar said: "When I first start-ed getting involved in Southern Baptist politics, everything was contentious and characterized by rancor. But then, slowly, something changed. David

Dockery started hosting these conferences at Union about Southern Baptists being united in evangelical conviction in moving beyond an era of battle talk and the 'us' vs. 'them' narrative. Dockery helped change the tone." Like Louis Armstrong or Duke Ellington, the magic is not just in the note choice but in how the music is played. Dockery himself would be the first to say the recovery of Baptist convictional collaboration was a wide-ranging, multi-institutional effort. But it's hard not to see his fingerprints on the whole business. There were the conferences at Union, the publication of his book *Building Bridges*, his fine work *Southern Baptist Consensus and Renewal*, his committee work on the SBC Great Commission Resurgence Task Team in 2010, among many other publications and denominational efforts. Further, this does not even cover his intense localism in which he tirelessly worked with associational and state Tennessee Baptist leaders to ensure Union was a leading partner in advocating Christian unity with key constituencies.

Over the years David Dockery crisscrossed the country speaking not only to Baptist schools but also to other institutions in Christian higher education who sought a preferred future for their institutions as part of a broader evangelical project. In sum he started a movement. It was real, and it is ongoing. If this volume in any way can help spread such sentiment, my collaborators and I would be grateful. In his career-defining work on the history of Baptist theology, James Leo Garrett, Dockery's mentor, spends considerable time talking about his protégé's contribution to the field.[8] In so doing, Dockery takes his place among great Baptist thinkers in recent history such as E. Y. Mullins, A. T. Robertson, W. T. Conner, and others as one of a handful of leaders in this generation who connected us to the traditions that have inspired us, built institutions that represent us, and changed the tone toward convictional civility in which Baptists and evangelicals show solidarity with one another "while we wait for the blessed hope and appearing of the glory of our great God and Savior, Jesus Christ" (Titus 2:13).

---

[8] James Leo Garrett, *Baptist Theology: A Four-Century Study* (Macon, GA: Mercer University Press, 2009), 704–10.

Tributes

A Word of Gratitude and Thanksgiving for David and Lanese Dockery

Daniel L. Akin

I t is a delightful assignment to express my appreciation, love, and respect for my brother and friend David Dockery. Charlotte and I have known him personally for more than twenty-five years. We served together briefly at Criswell College in the late 1980s, and he supported without reservation both my calling to Southern Seminary in 1996 and Southeastern Seminary in 2004. It was my privilege to follow him as academic vice president and dean of the School of Theology at Southern. His excellent work at that institution made my transition there an enjoyable and easy one. He did much of the "heavy lifting" before I arrived.

As is true of so many others, I could speak to his impact on my life as a stellar theologian. He models as well as anyone I know evangelical scholarship at its best. I could also talk at great length of how David has shown us what it means to be a Christian gentleman who is clear in his theological convictions and yet respectful toward all, including those with whom he disagrees. I could also extol his gifts as an administrator who has built one of the finest Christian universities anywhere in the world and the wonderful impact it had on two of my sons (Paul and Timothy) and one of my daughters-in-law (Kari). Each of their lives was impacted for the glory of God and the good of their souls by the incredible faculty and staff David has gathered at Union University. Bravo, my friend!

However, in my tribute to David Dockery, I want to be extremely personal. In fact this tribute will probably be different from any of the others you will read in this volume. You see, the Akin family will always have a special place in our hearts for the Dockery clan and with good reason. Let me explain.

In the fall of 1988, I left my position in a local church in Dallas, Texas, to join the faculty at Criswell College. It was a difficult decision, but my wife, Charlotte, and I were convinced it was the right decision. I should add that David's counsel and encouragement were factors in our decision. He was helpful.

Things got off to a fast and exciting start. We immediately fell in love with our colleagues and students. We felt right at home. Then one Monday evening, September 12, our lives were turned upside down. I had just sat down to watch the Dallas Cowboys play the Phoenix Cardinals. (As an aside, this would be Tom Landry's final year as the head coach of the Cowboys. Their record was a dismal 3–13 that season.) Suddenly one of our neighbor's sons ran into our house yelling, "Timothy has been hit by a car." Timothy is the youngest of our four sons and was three years old at the time. We ran outside to find him lying motionless in the street. We soon would learn that he had received serious bruising to his head and shoulder and that his leg was severely broken in two places. He would eventually be taken by helicopter to Parkland Hospital where he was rushed to their pediatric trauma unit. He would spend three weeks in the hospital (the majority of time at Baylor Hospital), several months in a body cast, and several more months in a leg cast. As I write this tribute to the Dockerys, Timothy is a wonderful husband and father of three sons, and he serves as a campus pastor at The Family Church in West Palm Beach, Florida. God was gracious!

When the accident occurred, we were forced into a whirlwind of activity and decisions. One was what do we do with the twins (Nate and Jon) who were school-age. Well, the cavalry arrived in the persons of David and Lanese Dockery! They showed up at the hospital and informed us that they were taking Nathan and Jonathan home with them. They further informed us, with grace but firmness, that they would return the boys to us when Timothy came home from the hospital. And that is what they did. For three weeks their home became our sons' home. They fed them, bathed them, clothed them, and took them to school and church along with their own three sons. They never asked for a penny and refused all our offers. They allowed us to give our full attention and focus to Timothy without any worries about Nate and Jon.

An incredible burden was lifted from our shoulders, and we never had to ask. The fact is David and Lanese did not give us the chance!

After Timothy came home from the hospital, they returned the boys as they promised. They loved on Timothy, hugged the twins good-bye and made their way home. It seemed like the most natural thing in the world to both of them.

As anyone could imagine, a special friendship exists to this day between the Akins and the Dockerys. The parents are dear friends and so are the seven sons. Through all of this I was able to see up close that David and Lanese Dockery live what they believe. They talk about loving others, and they do. They talk about serving others, and they do. My family was and has been the unique recipients of their grace and kindness. It is one of the reasons all the Akins love them so much, admire them so much, respect them so much, and appreciate them so much. They were there when we needed them most. David, Lanese, Jonathan, Ben, and Tim, we will never be able to say thank you enough for what you did for us in September 1988. Your friendship is a gift from God. We love you. Thank you.

Conviction, Courage, and Civility

Barry H. Corey

C onviction without courage goes nowhere. Courage without conviction goes anywhere. Conviction with courage goes somewhere. That "somewhere" becomes the place we dare to imagine in our deepest moments of moral strength. When civility unites conviction and courage, the force toward reaching that "somewhere" is so much greater. This is what David Dockery exemplifies in his life and work: a deep conviction for biblical authority and bold, unflinching leadership combined with a winsome, Christlike demeanor. He has made me a better leader by modeling these qualities in his presidency of Union University.

Conviction is the virtue that binds us to our most cherished and least changing beliefs. It grounds us in the truth and forms our ideological core. Courage is the virtue that calls us to bold action, reaching beyond the horizons of possibility. As Christians are called to be a present witness within our culture, this melding of conviction and courage guided by civility bears witness to the gospel.

In the twentieth century evangelicals and fundamentalists differed on matters of strategy and goals when it came to bearing witness to the gospel within our culture. Do we roll up our sleeves and engage the culture as redemptive voices as many from a more Reformed perspective argued? Or are our efforts merely tantamount to rearranging the deck chairs on the *Titanic*? Jesus' coming is imminent, so our main concern should be winning the lost and not involving ourselves in cultural redemption. Do we give up or do we take over?

This was the question many were asking during the rise of the neo-evangelicals in the 1940s and 1950s. Their answer was engagement rather than disengagement. They believed the walls of separation among Christian groups would begin to come down when Christian leaders recognized that their collective influence in the world would be greater together despite their theological or ecclesiastical differences. Harold John Ockenga, one of the prominent evangelical voices of the 1900s, together with many of his colleagues, argued the church must abandon its recent forebears' proclivity

> to withdraw from the culture and its institutions and commit themselves rather to the "principle of infiltration." . . . The reason for adopting such a strategy, Ockenga was convinced, was the importance of achieving four essential goals: the reform of society, the renewal of the church, a return to intellectual respectability, and the spread of the gospel around the globe.[1]

We have come a long way toward these four goals as evangelicals in this past century. Christians are in positions of public leadership at the highest levels, unapologetic about their faith. The church is being renewed as God raises leaders committed to his Word, who welcome the empowering work of the Holy Spirit and who are winsome in their witness. Evangelicals continue to emerge as thoughtful leaders and scholars, winning the widest academic respectability. And the gospel is raging like wildfire in the global south where the epicenter of Christianity is now moving.

At the same time hostility toward the Christian worldview is not necessarily abating, neither in the United States nor abroad. In fact a secularization of culture is underway in the West that tacks toward post-Christianity, and persecution of the Church globally, despite waves of renewal, has never been more rampant. Our task is to redouble our efforts to be people of conviction, courage, and civility, virtues our world needs to see in us and, through us, see the gospel. With deep-seated convictions from a theological foundation and confessional beliefs, we must approach the brokenness of the world without defensiveness, aloofness, or anger. To be responsible citizens and leaders in the communities God has called us to, we must be winsome, bold, neither elitist nor combative, more what we are for than against.

---

[1] Garth Rosell, *The Surprising Work of God: Harold John Ockenga, Billy Graham, and the Rebirth of Evangelicalism* (Grand Rapids: Baker, 2008), 162.

Like Moses humbly standing before that burning bush, may we learn to take off our shoes and understand that leadership and servanthood are about going barefoot, not putting on steel-toed boots to kick the heresy out of our brother or Jesus into our culture. Going barefoot, with openness to "the other," is the position Jesus and his disciples took as he washed their feet, taught them about being servants, and told them to go and do likewise. We must engage the culture with a deep conviction in truth but in a way that is meek, loving, graceful, and with an attractive fragrance. We need a firm center and soft edges. No saber rattling. No fist shaking. No scowled conversations. No voice raising. But we engage the culture with temperate tones by serving alongside and not casting stones from pedestals. It's what Peter meant in his words about defending our faith through conversations with the others God has placed in our lives: "But honor the Messiah as Lord in your hearts. Always be prepared to give a defense to anyone who asks you for a reason for the hope that is in you. However, do this with gentleness and respect" (1 Pet 3:15).

For centuries, followers of Christ have been addressing the world's brokenness with divine love through acts of compassion, creation of beauty through the arts, championing the great Christian intellectual tradition, and proclaiming the gospel in word and deed. This witness has been eroded when Christians take it upon themselves to respond with anger and acidic spirits. Equally condemnable as those who are angry are also those who are aloof. The indictment goes both ways. A number of years ago, Richard Mouw wrote a book on the subject of Christian civility, inspired by a line in one of Martin Marty's books: "The people who are good at being civil often lack strong convictions and people who have strong convictions often lack civility." What we need, Mouw writes, is "convicted civility."[2]

When conviction and courage are guided by civility, evangelicalism has the potential to look a lot different ten and twenty years down the road. It may well be bereft of political partisanship and no longer societally defined by cultural wars. Or we may be even more like aliens in a culture that is increasingly hostile to followers of Christ. If that is true, may we press forward even more with conviction, courage, and civility.

How we respond to the shifting of tectonic plates now underway will be the test of the church as it has been throughout the ages. With a world that is more accessible through technology, with a nation that is more ethnically

---

[2] Richard J. Mouw, *Uncommon Decency: Christian Civility in an Uncivil World*, rev. and expanded ed. (Downers Grove, IL: InterVarsity, 2010), 13–14. See Martin E. Marty, *By Way of Response* (Nashville: Abingdon, 1981), 81.

diverse, with the interreligious dialogue more at our doorstep than ever, with some of the faith's historic values under siege, Christians are being closely watched. Cultural complexities and global connectedness are part of our daily lives. Amid these changes, the truth of Scriptures even more must fortify our deepest convictions, fuel our courage, and call us to lives of gentleness. This means exercising the virtue of civility and exorcising the spirit of condescension. May we demonstrate the love of Jesus Christ by our faithful obedience to biblical conviction, by the strength of our Spirit-breathed courage, with the tone of Christian civility. May we engage the culture winsomely, boldly, and faithfully like David Dockery.

Winsome Champion for the Long Sweep of the Christian Intellectual Tradition

Philip W. Eaton

I remember the first time I met David Dockery. We were both serving on the national board of the Council for Christian Colleges and Universities. The board gathered each summer in a retreat setting in the high country of the Rocky Mountains of Colorado. David was a newer member than I was, as I remember; and as he began his tenure on the board, he seemed quiet and reserved, apparently willing to speak only when he felt he had something to say. But when he spoke, it became clear: people listened. My respect began to grow immediately.

This was my introduction to the style and character of this good man: well-spoken, respectful of others and process, anchored by deep conviction, a strong and steady voice at the table of Christian higher education. I was impressed.

And then Dave led devotions one morning that summer. That's when I came to know David Dockery as a man of substance. His remarks were carefully crafted, written out in fact. He talked with passion, clarity, and conviction about the mission of our Christian universities, but he also wanted to make clear that we must anchor our institutions on biblical moorings. I thought at the time, this is a man who knows and believes in our work but also a man who centers our work on the gospel of Jesus Christ. We need people of substance like this to lead our institutions. David Dockery is clearly that kind of leader.

Over the years I came to know David Dockery as one of the kindest people I know. So often Christian leaders tip over into stern dogmatism or ego-centered motivations. I found David always ready to encounter others with grace, kindness, and openness. This is real strength of character. I see David as a person who is open and curious toward others and the world.

Another thing stands out for me over time working with David Dockery. He communicates an abiding joy for learning: high learning, broad learning, deep learning, accessible learning. He has always been such a winsome champion for the long sweep of the Christian intellectual tradition. This is a powerful theme he wove into the fabric of Union University. I prize that so much in Dave. He reads widely. He reads deeply into the rich thought of our past. He refuses to screen out those positions that run contrary to his own conclusions. Rather, he revels in the opportunity to be shaped by the great thought of our long tradition.

I have watched David give himself wholly to Union University. I have had the privilege to visit his campus and speak to his faculty and students. I have been so impressed with the respect his campus community shows toward him and his leadership. He is a rock star on the campus and in the Jackson community. I am convinced that this respect and admiration are due to his being both a person of conviction and an encourager. He is a leader who builds up those with whom he works, a leader who builds a genuine sense of community for the university, a leader who wants the best for each person. People matter to him. He respects them, thanks them for their contribution, and counsels them.

But David is also a leader with vision. David will leave a huge mark on Union University. From the small town of Jackson, Tennessee, Dave has marshaled a great team of people to put this university on the map nationally. That takes vision. It takes a leader willing to articulate vision, to talk meaningful vision constantly and consistently. Indeed, I believe David crafted an attractive vision of university education, animated from the core by the gospel of Jesus Christ, and yet driven by a commitment for broad, deep, and vital learning. His commitment to the intellectual vibrancy and excellence of Union University provided just the right inspirational and aspirational energy for faculty, staff, and students to transform this university.

I am sure I am among a whole host of people who have received over time encouraging notes from David Dockery. This may not seem a legacy marker to some, but it is to me. Often these uplifting notes would come in the middle of the night, just part of the day for David. These notes have been so meaningful to me. He would always respond quickly to something I may have sent his way; but often, out of the blue, he would send a note to say, "Just thinking of you. May God bless you in your work at SPU." Something like that—that's the mark of a generous-hearted friend, a big person, a leader who spreads his care widely. That's the mark of a strong person willing to encourage the well-being and success of others.

David is one of those exceptional leaders motivated in his work not just for himself. David knew how to put Union on the map. He knew how to craft a vision for intellectual excellence, how to center this work with vibrant biblical orthodoxy. But his genuine commitment to people is finally the main legacy he will leave. David knew so well it takes both vision and people.

All of this adds up to just the right leader for Union, a leader as well for the national scene of Christian higher education. But I can think of no better way to characterize David Dockery than the encouragement the apostle Paul gives to all of us: "Put on heartfelt compassion, kindness, humility, gentleness, and patience. . . . Above all, put on love—the perfect bond of unity" (Col 3:12, 14).

These are the things that characterize the life and work of David Dockery. What a privilege it has been to know and work with this good man.

Irenic Conservative, Orthodox Baptist

Nathan A. Finn

I attended a Baptist college in the deep South where I majored in history and minored in Christianity. My professors in the latter department identified themselves as moderates and had disengaged from Southern Baptist denominational life during the previous decade. Theologically they were "center-left" on the spectrum of Southern Baptist thought at that time. In part because of my general interest in history and partly because of my professors' interpretations of recent denominational controversies, I became interested in modern Southern Baptist history. I read everything I could on what my pastor called the "Conservative Resurgence" and what my professors called the "Fundamentalist Takeover." I wrestled with my own convictions about all the debatable issues, especially biblical inerrancy, before coming to the conclusion that the conservative faith of my home church was still good enough for me.

Before I graduated from college, I already knew I wanted to pursue a Ph.D. and study some aspect of modern Baptist history or theology. I understood that I was choosing a vocation fraught with potential complications. Studying Baptist history is more than a merely academic exercise for a Southern Baptist; it can be politically tricky (ahem) in a postcontroversy world. As I continued reading widely in Baptist history and theology, I could not escape the feeling that many scholars were using history as an apologetic for their particular beliefs and/or were being far too polemical for a discipline that is theoretically more descriptive than prescriptive. Some historians were progressive individualists who framed Baptist identity as the forward march of personal liberty of conscience. Most doctrines seemed up for grabs, even doctrines I understood to be foundational to the faith. Other scholars were more conservative, like myself, but they sometimes came off as shrill and reactionary. They did not paint a winsome picture of what it means to be a theologically conservative Southern Baptist. Simply put, my moderate friends seemed more Christlike and friendly while my conservative friends seemed more orthodox and evangelistic.

As a collegian and wannabe Baptist historian, I found myself increasingly thankful for the works of David Dockery. I first became familiar with him through his book chapters and journal articles about Baptists and the doctrine of Scripture. Then I read chapters that recounted Baptist historical theology and opined about the future of Baptist thought. I also learned about the "Broadus-Robertson Tradition" and the theology of Herschel Hobbs and Millard Erickson. I then listened to some audio recordings of lectures Dockery had delivered at Southern Seminary, where I eventually began my M.Div. studies. I also read popular articles in magazines like *Christianity Today* and programmatic essays on Christian higher education. I began to recommend Dockery's writings to others.

I was surprised when I learned that Dockery was not a historian by profession; he seemed to understand recent Southern Baptist history and the history of Baptist thought as well as nearly any of the professional historians I was reading. He also seemed nice. What stood out most about Dockery was that he was never pugnacious. He approached some of the most controversial topics in Baptist history and theology as if neighbor love really matters. (The same was true of Dockery's friend Timothy George, who similarly influenced me in my vocational journey.) I told my pastor that I wished Union University had a divinity school so I could attend there for my seminary training! Alas, they did not.

By the time I began seminary, I knew there were different sorts of conservatives among Southern Baptists. I wanted to be a "David Dockery conservative" and use my scholarly gifts to interpret Southern Baptist history and theology but without being unnecessarily provocative or even polemical. Throughout my M.Div. and Ph.D. studies, I continued to read nearly everything Dockery wrote, even on topics that were of less personal or professional interest to me. In 2004, I finally had the chance to meet Dockery at the first Baptist Identity Conference at Union. I got to know him even better in the years after I joined the faculty at Southeastern Baptist Theological Seminary in 2007.

Since becoming a church historian, I have continued to be shaped by Dockery's influence. His 2009 book *Southern Baptist Consensus and Renewal* articulates almost exactly my own hope for the future of Southern Baptists. I have subsequently used that book in numerous Baptist history and Southern Baptist Convention courses at Southeastern Seminary. His contribution to the Southern Baptist conversations about the Great Commission Resurgence and Calvinism have been sane and measured—two words not often used in relation to those particular family conversations! Every SBC pastor and professor needs to read his essays or listen to his audio interviews on the nature of Southern Baptist cooperation. On a more personal note, he has been kind enough to take an interest in my own ministry, offering me wise counsel on several occasions. He also gave this young scholar two of my earliest writing opportunities when he invited me to contribute to books he was editing.

I hope Dockery will be able to write even more than he has in the past (which is pretty impressive). I believe he can still teach Southern Baptists much about pursuing a winsome Baptist orthodoxy, the importance of thoughtful engagement with both other evangelicals and the Christian intellectual tradition, and the ongoing relevance of intentionally Christian higher education. I am confident that whatever topics Dockery chooses to pursue in the coming years, he will do so out of a spirit of convictional civility. I think many Southern Baptists could use a bit more of that spirit, wherever our own interests might lie—myself included. If we hope to enjoy the sort of fruitful future that Dockery has proposed for us, then moving forward we will need as many "David Dockery conservatives" as we can get.

A Civil "Wedge" in the World

George H. Guthrie

O ne crisp, blustery evening last autumn, my wife and I sat cozily in a candlelit evensong service at Trinity College in Cambridge, England. The chapel, built during the sixteenth-century reigns of Mary and Elizabeth I, stands majestically like a stately old queen, her jewelry gold trim and dark wood, her makeup an elaborately painted ceiling, her feet shod with black-and-white marble, her frame draped with stained glass, and her voice a massive organ rising up over the entrance to the chapel proper. The liturgy, rich with Scripture counterpointed by soaring choral pieces, created a warm, welcoming space for worship.

As I sat in the service, Scripture poignantly told the gospel to the little crowd and the choir of mostly secular, young university students, speaking of sacrifice, forgiveness, and resurrection. Here in the heart of post-Christian England, my mind briefly stepped down out of the pew into the quiet of evensong, wandering quickly out the doors. Like a ghost my memory ran through the streets of Cambridge and to the many other cathedrals, chapels, and churches my family had visited in the city and throughout Great Britain over the previous months. And I was struck with an idea.

As someone who spends much of my life walking the dusty streets of the New Testament world, with its house-church groups embodying the new covenant temple of God, I embrace the aesthetic glory and the rich history of Europe's cathedrals and chapels while remaining theologically reserved on their true value for the advancement of the kingdom in their time and place. After all, as a Baptist my roots are more nonconformist. What do we have to do with the grand monuments of royals and priests? Yet these beautiful, old buildings, set down in the world, draped in such beauty and crafted with astonishing mechanical expertise—along with the ongoing rhythms they house, rhythms of evensongs and liturgies and chapel bells pealing out over Britain—continue to occupy a space in the world, a presence that presses into college schedules and camera lenses, tourist itineraries and radio waves, and the consciousness of normal, everyday people walking the cobblestones. Such buildings, filled with such ministries, are like a wedge in the world, always there, by their existence making space, garnering attention for God like smooth-stone giants confronting a culture that thinks itself moved on from theology.

Wedges make space. One of the best things I can say about my friend and colleague David Dockery is that God has crafted him, like the cathedrals of Europe, as "a wedge in the world." Not a log-shattering, wood-splintering, force-driven-no-matter-the-effect type of wedge. No, like a stately cathedral or a humble chapel, he often sits to the side quietly, unobtrusively offering a convictional but civil voice. But David Dockery constitutes a wedge with massive intelligence, conviction, and vision on the "thick" end, balanced on the "thin" end by a razor-sharp integrity, impressive people skills, and a disarming humility and civility. The thin end makes a way into places of impact. The thick end demands expanding space, riveted attention. God has seen fit to craft David Dockery as a massively effective wedge, a penetrating "space maker" in our world. And in being God's wedge, he has been used to make spaces for those of us at Union University for a while.

At Union David has been used of God to foster a theologically informed conversation on the integration of orthodox Christian faith and university-level learning. That conversation, initially a good idea that flecked the fringes of our praxis as a university, now weaves thick threads through our institutional fabric. As David's national influence has grown over the years, expanded in part by convocation addresses, guest lectureships, published works, and visionary administrative leadership, his contribution to the broader discussion in Christian higher education has been recognized as significant by other leaders, especially throughout North America. By God's grace David has made a significant space for the integration of faith and learning at Union, and that conversation opened up spaces in other places.

Tapping of the "great Christian intellectual tradition" as a compass for our own program of academic endeavor, however, has been carried out not with a cold, austere intellectualism but rather with a warm, Great Commandment heart. In other words David Dockery, by his example and his authentic Christian leadership, has made a space for vibrant, authentic Christian spirituality, a spirituality in which we love, praise, and thank God unashamedly. Rather than a dichotomous, "two-sphere" approach to university life, by which heart and head are held apart, David has shown us a truly integrated life of intellectual pursuit in which we love the Lord our God with all we are, following Christ as a much-loved and loving Lord into our disciplines, as we sit in our house and as we walk along the way, for the good of our university, the church, and the world.

And this genuine love for God has fostered Christian community, a meaningful, relational context in which we live, and move, and have our being. People who are thriving spiritually, relating well to their God, tend to relate better to one another, making for a productive and happy community. We are not a perfect community, so the community must be "grace filled," as David has said so often. But grace has to be received before it can be given. So a community grounded in the gospel should know better how to be patient and redemptive with one another. As God's gracious wedge in our place and time, David has modeled such grace and thus made space for a healthy, thriving community.

Of course, like a marathoner leaning into a long and difficult race, a thriving community must see clearly where it is going. In other words it must have a crystal clear *vision*, an understanding of why it exists and how individual gifts contribute to that mission. Here too David has played the wedge—a visionary wedge. For David Dockery has the uncanny ability to discern peoples' gifts and to facilitate those gifts to the advancement of the mission of the university and, ultimately, for the cause of Christ. For me personally David has crafted a space for my gifts to flourish, for which I am deeply grateful. A number of years ago I had come to a crossroads in my university "career." At that crossroads I was tempted to go deeper into administration. Yet that crossroads corresponded with my first research leave. The space of the leave, in which I was immersed in research and writing in Cambridge, England, for several months, reignited my *love* for research and writing (I had been doing both alongside administration) and reminded me that my primary gifts are those of teacher/communicator. David graciously encouraged me to follow my gifts and passions. Now eight years later on a second research leave, I am thriving in my space and place in the university and the world, thankful for the impact of David Dockery on my life and ministry. Great Christian leaders make space for *others* to thrive as God's wedges in the world, who can then probe and push against the narrowness of human experience, making a place for the life-expanding gospel in all the dark corners of the globe.

For after all, hasn't the gospel made a space for us in God's family and given us a distinct mission in the world? And here we find the foundation of who David S. Dockery is and what he is about. He lives and works as a powerful, uniquely crafted wedge, a space maker, in God's world because God's gospel has wedged its way deeply into his heart. Like the liturgy in Trinity Chapel, Cambridge, which rhythmically sings out the real song at the heart of the universe, the gospel sings at the center of David's existence. I can give no greater tribute.

Wholehearted Conviction and Winsome Civility

Barbara C. McMillin

Having had the great blessing of serving at Union University under the leadership of David S. Dockery for the majority of his tenure there, I brought with me to the presidency of Blue Mountain College a model for Christ-centered excellence in higher education administration. All who know him or know of him will agree that David Dockery has set the bar high, demonstrating for each of us who hold a position of leadership the traits that define the casting of extraordinary visions and the establishment of exemplary values. Amounting to many more than can be articulated in the space offered here, those traits in combination produce what the writers of this *Festschrift* gratefully recognize as David Dockery's wholehearted conviction and winsome civility.

On the occasion of my inauguration as president of Blue Mountain College, I was greatly honored by David Dockery's presence and greatly inspired by his delivery of the inaugural charge, which concluded with the admonition to "keep the main thing the main thing"—a fitting summary to a charge focused on pursuing wholeheartedly the convictions on which our faith-based institutions were founded. In a culture confounded by relativism, Dr. Dockery has consistently reminded Christian leaders of our commitment to that which is "enduringly relevant," namely that "God is more important than we are, that the future life is more important than this one, and that a right view of God gives significance and security to our lives."[1] The absence of such "healthy theological commitments"—failure to keep the main thing the main thing—exposes institutions and individuals to the capricious waves and winds depicted in Ephesians 4:14.[2]

In his charge to me personally, to the many other leaders mentored by Union University's fifteenth president, and to the countless others who have felt his influence, the substance of David Dockery's confessional foundation remains steadfast: "belief in a triune God" and "in one mediator between God and humanity, the man Christ Jesus who came to this earth as God incarnate; . . . a belief in a fully authoritative Bible, and the message of salvation by grace through faith made known therein."[3] Upon this unshakeable foundation David Dockery has unapologetically and wholeheartedly invested his life in service to Christian higher education and to the kingdom of God.

For a wholehearted conviction to thrive, it must be accompanied by an equal complement of civility: the ability to communicate one's convictions in a way that is winsome and not worrisome, congenial not combative. In clear possession of such winsomeness, David Dockery has taught us by example how to stand firm while standing "side by side with a clarion call to biblical truth." He has taught us by example to "hold hands and serve together with brothers and sisters who disagree on secondary and tertiary matters of theology and work together toward a common good to extend our shared work around the world and advance the kingdom of God." He has reminded us that "we can relate to one another in love and humility, bringing about true fellowship and community not only in orthodoxy but orthopraxy before a watching world."[4] Attempts to relate to one another in less positive, less respectful ways jeopardize our message while calling into question our desire to love our neighbor as we love ourselves.

For eighteen years David Dockery has led Union University, partnering with its trustees, faculty, staff, students, and alumni to grow an institution recognized by all for its commitment to being excellence driven, Christ centered, people focused, and future directed. He has, by God's great faithfulness, persevered in advancing the "Christian intellectual tradition," a concept and a phrase present in the professional lexicon of leaders and thinkers in Christian

---

[1]   David S. Dockery, *Christian Leadership Essentials: A Handbook for Managing Christian Organizations* (Nashville: B&H, 2011), 344.
[2]   Ibid.
[3]   Ibid., 345.
[4]   Ibid.

higher education largely because of David Dockery's insight and eloquence. Such phraseology illustrates the manner and extent to which Dr. Dockery has shaped even the way we speak about what we do on a daily basis. From David Dockery we have learned much about loving God with our minds, including the words we use to describe how we are to fulfill this command. Thank you, David Dockery, for inspiring us through your wholehearted conviction to "think Christianly" and through your winsome civility to live lives and build communities that are "grace-filled." We are eternally grateful.

Cultural Warrior, Intellectual Strategist, and Recognized Visionary

Carol Swain

I f we are to change America and regain what is left of our Judeo-Christian heritage, we must have men and women who understand the signs of our times and are bold enough to engage our culture using frontal and subtle tactics. In David Dockery there is a mild-mannered countenance borne of his theological training and knowledge that disarms and charms those with whom he disagrees.

I met Dr. Dockery during the heat of the battle for religious freedom at Vanderbilt University, where I am a professor of political science and of law. In 2011, Vanderbilt adopted a "nondiscrimination" policy that stripped students and, later, faculty of religious exemptions that had always existed at the university. The policy meant that Christian organizations could no longer require their leaders to share their faith, nor could they ask leaders of Christian organizations to affirm a belief in Jesus Christ as Lord and Savior or to perform the functions of leading a Bible study or a worship service. Dr. Dockery played a pivotal role in getting the Tennessee Baptist Convention and the Baptist organization on the Vanderbilt campus to reverse its earlier compromising stance and join the solidarity movement. He stood with us, and for that I'll always be grateful. That movement involved a group of thirteen to fifteen Christian organizations that made the painful decision to leave campus and forgo official university recognition rather than compromise their core values and principles.

David Dockery is a visionary that God has used mightily over the past thirty years or so. His book *Renewing Minds: Serving Church and Society Through Higher Education* should be required reading for every Christian trustee, parent, and student who would like to understand what a Christian university can do to impact the world for Christ. In this influential book Dockery covers every aspect that should concern those of us who would like to see minds and hearts changed as we strive for relevance in a global world. If we can internalize and apply the wisdom of this learned man, we will be much further along in the battle to save our nation and train the next generation of Christian leaders.

Dr. Dockery's edited anthology *Faith and Learning: A Handbook for Christian Higher Education* is a compilation of chapters of different disciplines written by some of the best scholarly minds in the country. These pieces give a deeper understanding of how their respective authors' particular areas of expertise fit into the larger enterprise of educating students with specialized knowledge comfortably coexisting with Christian faith traditions. Whether the university is secular or Christian, there is a place for faculty aware of a God-directed career, where their faith and knowledge can enhance the educational experiences of the young people God has placed under their care, where the synergy surrounding that faith and knowledge can energize the next generation of leaders.

The man and his work have the ability to encourage, uplift, and leave one in awe. As the commencement speaker at Union University in 2012, I was able to visit the campus and meet with faculty and students and see the work up close. It was a deeply moving experience to see the influence of Christ and Christian principles and values undergirding a world-class education. In these days when so many once-Christian colleges and universities embrace secularization, it is refreshing to see Union University's effectiveness in integrating faith and learning into a powerful model that could be replicated on other campuses. Union University's Christ-centered influence has had and will hopefully continue to have a world-changing impact as its students graduate and take leadership positions across the globe.

What Dr. Dockery has perfected is a form of engagement with the broader culture that emphasizes a Christian worldview and how that worldview can influence and galvanize Christ followers. As Dr. Dockery reminds us in *Renewing Minds: Serving Church and Society Through Christian*

Higher Education, everyone has a worldview, even the most ardent atheist. A Christian worldview must answer the following questions:

- Where did we come from?
- Who are we?
- What has gone wrong with the world?
- What solutions can be offered to deal with these challenges?

As Dr. Dockery points out, the answer begins with our "confessions that we believe in God the Father, Maker of heaven and earth" (The Apostles' Creed). We recognize that "by Him all things hold together" (Col 1:17).

It will be exciting to see the next God-directed assignment entrusted to Dr. Dockery. In the meantime I expect we will be continually blessed by more of his seminal books and articles and hopefully his leadership in higher education.

Activist for Racial Reconciliation

Kimberly Thornbury

D avid Samuel Dockery is a faithful son of Alabama. But he demonstrated an entirely different meaning to this designation when, in 1970, he stood alongside African-American brothers and sisters as a high school senior at the height of racial tension in the South. When Dockery began the second semester of his senior year in Birmingham, Alabama, the courts ordered his local school system to desegregate. As the Friday, May 29, 1970, edition of the *Birmingham News* read, "All the students—black and white—in the 11th and 12th grades were asked to attend Fairfield High School." Desegregation was not well received.

A modern college student who has seen the movie *Remember the Titans* might (wrongly) assume that after a few months of challenges, a newly desegregated community would ultimately rally together and unify. However, this was not the case as Dockery entered his final few months of high school. Like most schools in the South (especially Birmingham, Alabama), desegregation was a long and painful process. Dockery experienced this conflict firsthand, and as student body president of his high school, he would have to make a leadership decision few student body presidents have had to face. The same article in the *Birmingham News* explains the culminating conflict that occurred on graduation day, when the white students and their parents boycotted graduation with their black classmates. The Alabama state superintendent Dr. Ernest Stone recalls receiving a call the morning of the graduation that explained, as he described, a "white boycott" of the school's graduation. This separate graduation was organized by parents at the local Forest Hills Baptist Church, and catered to 110 seniors, all white. "Fairfield High School seniors picked up their diplomas at separate graduate exercises Thursday night—one school-sponsored and the other, at a church, described as 'private,'" the article reports.

The teenaged David Dockery, however, chose not to participate in the boycott. The school-sponsored graduation addressed 115—all black except for Dockery and thirteen others (mostly women). In the midst of what must have been enormous peer pressure, Dockery chose to do the right thing. Perhaps Dockery thought back to the time when he was ten years old and heard about the bombing of the Birmingham church, killing four girls and injuring twenty-two other people on September 15, 1963. His parents drove him past the burned building, and he "couldn't quite grasp that a sacred place like that would be the object of such hatred and devastation." By God's grace Dockery was propelled to "seek to become an agent of grace and reconciliation."[1]

Dockery went on to pastor a multiethnic church in Brooklyn, New York, in the early 1980s. In the 1990s, Dockery served as dean at The Southern Baptist Theological Seminary in Louisville, Kentucky. In that role, "he helped the school of theology recruit its first two black faculty members."[2] As president of Union University, Dockery continued his work, including, but not limited to: establishing a center for racial reconciliation, supporting a thriving multicultural student group, and significantly increasing the number of minority students who attended the university. Because of his active role in establishing multiethnic relationships and partnerships and because of his continued work including new lectureships, symposiums, and student groups on the campus, the NAACP invited Dockery to deliver the 2009 plenary address at the annual West Tennessee NAACP chapter. Dockery was the first Caucasian to be given this honor. In 2013, Dockery chaired an intercultural ministerial educational summit, focused on "how Southern Baptists can help prepare believers called to ministry from non-Anglo churches."[3]

Despite narratives that might suggest Dockery's Southern Baptist background should mitigate against his involvement with the Civil Rights movement, it was actually his deep commitment to evangelism and congregationalism that drove his passion for justice. A "cradle-roll Baptist" who

[1]   Baptist Press, October 4, 2013.
[2]   Ibid.
[3]   Ibid.

dedicated his life to the denomination, Dockery, even as a boy, began to connect the dots between racial reconciliation and sharing the good news of Jesus. Although the language is perhaps now outdated, the song "Jesus Loves the Little Children" made a real difference in his nascent worldview. If Jesus loves all the little children regardless of race, he reasoned, then I must too. Solidarity with God's chosen people, visibly through baptism, corporate worship, and the Lord's Supper, framed the way Dockery saw his responsibilities toward others. If you can imagine yourself singing and responding to the preached word with a brother or sister, then you should be able to cross a graduation platform with them as well.

On a personal note, I was able to see Dr. Dockery's passion for racial reconciliation firsthand, not as a "higher education trend of the decade" or stemming from "political correctness" but as a part of his administrative priorities from the beginning, with consistent and tireless work toward a preferred future for the campus. I observed a man who cleared off papers from his office every night and first thing each morning took out stationery and pen to begin his day at that desk writing (at least) three thank-you notes to others. He was always one to deflect praise and recognize others for their work. Doing the right thing with and for others is one of many qualities that define Dr. Dockery as one of the greatest leaders in our time.

Friend, Mentor, and Guide

Jon R. Wallace

D avid Dockery is one of Christian higher education's most significant and influential leaders of the last fifty years. Great leaders like David begin with the end in mind and see the journey as an interwoven series of teachable moments for themselves and for those whom they lead. I am deeply influenced by David's leadership and continue to benefit from his mentoring. For the last fourteen years, David has spoken into my life as the president of Azusa Pacific University. His wise counsel and thoughtful discernment helped shape me as a leader and APU as a Christian university. David's impact on my life encompasses roles as friend, mentor, and guide.

In summer 2001, Gail and I joined the CCCU New Presidents' program, where we met other presidential couples who were new to this journey as well as veterans. Immediately I was drawn to David's quiet wisdom, calm demeanor, and encouraging vision for our call. That night Gail and I requested David and Lanese Dockery to serve as our mentors. The next day the Dockerys became our official guides to the adventure of presidential leadership.

From the onset Gail and I experienced transparent, warm, and inviting friendship from David and Lanese. That friendship grew over the next fourteen years, strengthened by mutual travel, common challenges, and similar stages of family and life. To be David's friend is to be given a "backstage pass" to new and interesting people, ideas, and experiences. He captured the spirit of our friendship and revealed the genuineness of his character when he introduced me as a new president to others he knew. "This is Jon Wallace, the president at Azusa Pacific University, and my friend." *And my friend.* Those words connected us whenever I had a question, a challenge, or a fear. My deep and abiding friendship with David is one of the great gifts that has come through my call to presidential leadership.

The reason he was such an impactful mentor was due to the different paths David and I took to the presidency. Mine came through student life and university operations, his through scholarship and academic leadership. David's patient mentoring on the importance of academic excellence, scholarship that informs the classroom, and the role of faculty in accomplishing the mission of the university transformed my leadership. Several years ago he sent me the working draft of a book he was writing. As I read his view of Christian higher education, this statement struck a chord: "Our Christian colleges and universities should reflect the life of Christ and shine the light of truth." I was in the middle of a ten-day backpacking trip and pondered those simple, but powerful words: "reflect the life of Christ and shine the light of truth." Upon my return I called David, affirming the importance of his manuscript and asking if I could borrow that statement for APU. To reflect the life of Christ and shine the light of truth serves as the foundation of our vision for accomplishing the mission of APU. In essence, David's model of mentoring makes available the best of his thinking and allows it to be used by God in others.

David serves, too, as a guide for me. An expanded role of mentoring, he provides thoughtful feedback and wise counsel for the path ahead. Senior leaders must often navigate unfamiliar and precarious paths while moving an institution and its stakeholders forward to accomplish the mission. A familiar phrase of advice from him is, "We often overestimate what can be accomplished in a year and underestimate what can be accomplished in five years." This represents the heart of his gift of guidance: to see the journey in light of the finish line. As guide he led the APU board of trustees in conversation on the history of evangelicalism and then helped the university administration and faculty consider fidelity to our Christ-centered mission. Further, he generously shared his insights with us about a thoughtful approach to civic engagement and the model of convicted civility as a basis for Christ followers in the public square. I believe this may well be one of his most important guiding conversations.

I trust these brief words convey my thankfulness for the gift of Dr. David Dockery as friend, mentor, and guide. He remains for me and those who stand on the well-lit path of his influence, a leader "who reflects the life of Christ and shines the light of truth."

David, as one of many who have been shaped by your leadership excellence, my deepest thanks. And as always, I look forward to our next conversation.

Faithful Servant

James Emery White

Ray Boltz wrote a song called "Thank You." It goes, "Thank you, for giving to the Lord. I am a life that was changed." I can only imagine the number of people who could sing those words to David Dockery. I know that God used David to change my life.

We first met on the campus of Southern Seminary when he was a wet-behind-the-ears New Testament professor and I an even wetter Ph.D. student. He asked me to become his "fellow" (translation: "grader"), giving me the rare distinction of being a Garrett Fellow in both theology (which I already was) and New Testament.

We became fast friends. He then advocated my hiring to become the leadership consultant for preaching and worship for what used to be the Baptist Sunday School Board and is now LifeWay Christian Resources. As an editor for Broadman and Holman, he selected my doctoral dissertation for publication, a rare honor for any academic, which opened doors around the world. But he opened the first one by then inviting me to be part of a team to Russia shortly after the fall of the Berlin Wall to teach at the Moscow Theological Institute. It was my first overseas trip.

When he became president of Union University, he invited me to serve on various councils, preach in chapels, and serve students and faculty. As I wrote books and built a church, David planted the seed in many minds—such as Chuck Colson's—that I would be a good seminary president. And indeed, I became the fourth president for Gordon-Conwell Theological Seminary.

Throughout many years David has been a friend, counselor, and bene-factor. And I am just one story of hundreds that could walk down a similar path of memories. But most of all, to all of us, David has been a model. This is important. I've met too many leaders who are not who they appear to be. They have names, reputations, publications, and platforms, but often absent are character and virtue. I can tell you that the David you meet, the David you see, the David you read, the David you heard, is the David who is.

I can think of no higher compliment or honor.

And what has he modeled?

- He has modeled commitment to marriage and family.
- He has modeled doctrinal orthodoxy.
- He has modeled a winsome and compelling cultural and theological apologetic.
- He has modeled an irenic spirit in a day of fractious division.
- He has modeled selfless, servant leadership that sets others up for impact and influence.
- But most of all, he has been a model of spiritual authenticity.

When we were in Russia, one night a group of us went to the famed Bolshoi Ballet. It was a wonderful evening but long, and we were tired. Yet after we took the subway back to where we were staying, the students said, "Come and let us celebrate." I wanted to go to bed. David wanted to celebrate. So I went along. Then I found out what David seemed to know. They wanted to gather in the dining room and sing hymns and worship God. And we did, late into the night, with more passion and sincerity than I have ever experi-enced. It didn't matter that we didn't sing in Russian—we worshipped God together. There was no audience, no cameras, just a group of Christian men in a kitchen in Moscow at the end of a long day. And no one worshipped more heartily than David.

This *Festschrift* honors Dr. David S. Dockery, celebrating his comple-tion of eighteen years serving as president of Union University. It is titled *Convictional Civility*. I write to honor a larger span than that. And I would title it "Faithful Servant."

Generous, Wise, and Humble

John D. Woodbridge

On one occasion while I was recovering from surgery, the doorbell rang at our home. Flowers arrived to brighten the day. More than the flowers themselves, the thought that someone remembered what I had just experienced generated a certain buoyancy, a warm feeling. Unfortunately in this particular instance, the florist failed to leave a card that identified the individual who had sent the flowers. Thereafter ensued detective work with the florist who eventually identified the sender as Dr. David Dockery, the president of Union University.

To me the flowers represented clear evidence attesting to Dr. Dockery's caring Christian spirit. I later learned that Dr. Dockery's thoughtfulness and graciousness in remembering to send a word of congratulations to a colleague for a new publication, a bravo to a student athlete for a job well done, a note of encouragement and comfort to a person who had experienced a loss, are near legendary. Undoubtedly Dr. Dockery's example has stimulated others to think through more fully how to love their neighbors better in showing concern for them in the name of Christ.

It is one thing to be a generous Christian person; it is another to be a wise and humble Christian. Now if you find a believer who is generous, wise, and humble, then watch out world. Such a person is Dr. Dockery, a genuinely humble Christian leader whose innovative plans are not couched in self-aggrandizing motivations but in a desire to bring glory to Christ. Other Christians will rally to that leader's vision and plans because they do not see a self-promoting "I" between his eyes. Rather they become happily convinced the leader really does want to lift up Christ and is resolutely kingdom focused. Undoubtedly Dr. Dockery's remarkable success as a Christian educator and university president has stimulated others to want to emulate his example as a generous, wise, and humble servant leader.

Now it is one thing that Dr. Dockery is a generous, wise, and humble Christian. But he is also like Christian in John Bunyan's *Pilgrim's Progress* in weathering the struggles, toils, and disappointments associated with this pilgrimage called life. Sometimes the pilgrim faces daunting adversities that can be dispiriting on the journey to his or her celestial home. But like Bunyan's Christian, Dr. Dockery has persevered and overcome obstacles by trusting in the Lord's loving providence. He has remembered to focus on Christ during the journey. He has continued faithfully to proclaim the gospel message of justification by faith alone. Not wanting to rely on the arm of the flesh, through prayer he has called on the Holy Spirit's power for strength. He has trusted in the enduring promises of Holy Scripture. He has experienced the peace and joy of his salvation in Christ.

Dr. Dockery has other traits that need to be lauded. As his family members can attest, he is a loving father and husband and is a lot of fun to be around. Moreover he has a passion for sports.

One thing I have not fully fathomed about Dr. Dockery is the depth of his love for Alabama football. Not only does Dr. Dockery love the Crimson Tide; he may secretly think everyone else should. How do I know this? On one occasion Dr. Dockery with missionary zeal apparently decided he should coach me to say with feeling, "Roll Tide." Now I too am interested in sports and have exhibited irrational and undying loyalty to the feckless Chicago Cubs. But I have not been of the mind to encourage my neighbors to say, "Wait until next century," the hope fans of the Cubs have been forced to embrace.

Given Dr. Dockery's friendship, I did learn to say "Roll Tide." Perhaps my acquiescence to Dr. Dockery's coaching was due to the unexpected pleasure of rooting for a winning sports team, an experience diehard Cubs fans have seldom enjoyed.

Little doubt exists that today Dr. David Dockery continues to serve the Church of Jesus Christ as one of her most trusted and wise Christian educators and theologians. He provides a wonderful example for all of us of a Christian who is generous, wise, and humble. For Dr. Dockery's faithful, kingdom-focused ministry we give the Lord heartfelt thanks.

Learning from a Master

Carl Zylstra

A veteran college president spoke at my own presidential inauguration. He compared the college presidency to being sexton at a cemetery. "In both cases," he said, "there are a lot of people underneath you—but nobody's moving." Indeed, it didn't take me long to discover he was right. A college president doesn't stand atop a chain of command and just bark out orders. Rather, the key to an effective presidency is recognizing that your overarching task is to unite diverse constituencies in pursuit of a common goal and to do so primarily by vision and suasion.

The problem a new president like me had was this: Where was I going to find a model who demonstrated how that could be done. Gratefully it took only a month for me to meet David Dockery who, although a new college president himself, embodied the combination of deep conviction, expansive vision, and Christian graciousness that enabled him to accomplish in a remarkable way that central task of a college president: building a vigorous institution and a thriving campus in pursuit of a vibrant mission.

What I learned from David Dockery was the importance of patient listening combined with perceptive filtering. He knew that other people had great ideas, and he wanted to hear them all. But he also knew that most of their ideas, frankly, weren't as good as his own. However, rather than dismissively shutting his ears once he knew they were on the wrong track, David was able to hear them out and then strategize ways to incorporate them into a plan that really would work.

But David Dockery also demonstrated how to maintain his leadership convictions and insights even when hitting roadblocks that make implementation of those insights impossible, at least for the moment. While he knew he was right, he was not about to squander his leadership capital on ventures that would not gain others' support.

Plus, when good things did happen, David was more than willing to let the results speak for themselves rather than try to take credit for having brought them about. The transformation of the Union University campus and curriculum is astounding and an inspiration that I and other leaders have scrambled to keep pace with. Indeed, the growth of many Christian and other private colleges can be attributed in no small part to trying to keep Union's taillights at least in sight!

That means, of course, that President Dockery realized it was more important that people be amazed at the results of the efforts he led rather than be impressed with him as the leader. His Christian graciousness of spirit grew out of a true humility of character. True, David Dockery never tired of tooting Union's horn. He might have garnered even greater recognition, however, had he, at least on occasion, tooted his own horn as well.

In short, David Dockery knew how to be the smartest guy in the room (and he usually was) and then use that position not to demean or demoralize but rather to empower for kingdom goals.

Plus, he really understood those kingdom goals. As a New Testament scholar, he built his remarkable organizational leadership firmly on the deep biblical principles that his outstanding scholarship developed and which he freely shared in a torrent of publications, speeches, and sermons. David Dockery just wasn't all that into institution building. Rather, he was totally into biblical faithfulness that, he was convinced, Christ could use to build his own kingdom.

In that regard David Dockery was critical in helping keep the Christian college movement on course. In a time when theologically shaped leaders were sometimes denigrated as a leftover of medievalism and being replaced by management technicians, he boldly stood against the tide. But he did so not by railing from a soapbox but by modeling from the card table in his living room where his publications were given birth.

But perhaps the most important lesson David Dockery taught was that an effective leader must always be the hardest worker in the organization. There's a misconception that when someone reaches the top of the leadership pyramid, it's time to rest on the labors of those below. But that was never President Dockery's approach.

He embodied that characteristic most dramatically in response to the tornado that struck the heart of Union's campus on February 5, 2008. Like every good leader his first concern was the well-being of the students in the collapsed buildings. Like truly extraordinary leaders he also made sure to ask, even before that dreadful night was over, "What do we have to do to make sure this institution's mission is strengthened, not destroyed, by this disaster?" But only an incomparable leader will have the answer to that question firmly in hand even before dawn the following day. And only an astounding leader like David Dockery will then spend the next four days, literally without sleep, to make sure a plan to accomplish the new vision is not only formulated but actually underway before the week is over.

Now some highly energetic leaders dispirit those who observe them because of their own inability to maintain the pace the leader sets. However, over the years as we would watch David Dockery's example—filtered through his own humble, steady spirit—we, instead, were stimulated to work all the harder lest we be left behind in that joyful project of unstinting service that David Dockery led and embodied.

Through it all he always remained a master teacher who knew the difference between scholarship that simply intrigues and wisdom that truly transforms. He showed us that a real visionary always believes that what exists today truly may be different from what ought to be tomorrow. And maybe most important of all, he showed us that for the big picture to be realized, the details simply had to be done right.

Was he a perfect leader? Of course not (some wags would point to the fact that Union University still doesn't yet have a football team as example number one!). But he was a loyal friend to those who walked—or, perhaps better, scrambled to run—with him on the journey. And because he was, those who accompanied him were motivated to do their best in their own places of service throughout the Christian college world. It is not an exaggeration to say that the movement of Christian higher education simply could not be what it is today without the example, encouragement, and leadership of David Dockery.

David S. Dockery: Professional Highlights (1984–2014)[1]

I. Academic Appointments

Trinity International University
President (2014–)

Union University
President and University Professor of Christian Thought (1996–2014; also given honorary title of Chancellor for 2014 and beyond)

The Southern Baptist Theological Seminary
Senior Vice President for Academic Administration (1993–96)
Dean, School of Theology (1992–96)
Faculty appointments in New Testament and Theology (1988–96)

Criswell College
Professor of Theology and New Testament (1984–88)

II. Select Listing of Publications

(The listings are not exhaustive but are representative of the scope of the work by David S. Dockery.)

A. Articles

"Southern Baptist Theology in the Twentieth Century: A Denomination Coming of Age." *Southwestern Journal of Theology* 54, no. 2 (Spring 2012).

"Global Awareness and Engagement: New Opportunities for Christian Higher Education." *Pro Rege* (June 2011).

"The History of New Testament Studies at Southern Seminary." *Southern Baptist Journal of Theology* 13 (Spring 2009).

"Are We There Yet?" *Touchstone* (October 2005).

"The Crisis of Scripture in Southern Baptist Life: Reflections on the Past, Looking to the Future." *Southern Baptist Journal of Theology* 9 (Spring 2005).

---

[1] Compiled by Cindy Meredith.

"Toward a Theology for Baptist Higher Education." *The Southern Baptist Educator* (October 2004).

"Christian Doctrine for a Post-Everything World." *Southwestern News* (Fall 2003).

"A Theology for the Church." *Midwestern Journal of Theology* 1, no. 1 (2003).

"Modern and Christian: How to Think with the Mind of Christ." *Books And Culture* (July/August 2002).

"A Theology of Baptism." *Southwestern Journal of Theology* 43 (Spring 2001).

"Integrating Faith and Learning: An Unapologetic Case for Christian Higher Education." *Faith And Mission* 18, no. 1 (2000).

"Is Revelation Prophecy or History?" *Christianity Today* (October 25, 1999).

"Interpreting the New Testament for Preaching." *Faith And Mission* 12 (1995).

"Introduction to Galatians." *Review and Expositor* 91 (1994).

"The History of Pre-critical Biblical Interpretation." *Faith and Mission* 10 (1992).

"A Theology of Acts." *Criswell Theological Review* 5, no. 1 (1990).

"Acts 6–12: The Christian Movement Beyond Jerusalem." *Review and Expositor* 87 (1990).

"Millard Erickson: Baptist and Evangelical Theologian." *Journal of The Evangelical Theological Society* 32 (1989).

"A Reformation Day Sermon." *Preaching* (October 1989).

"Author? Reader? Text? Toward a Hermeneutical Synthesis." *Theological Educator* 37 (1988).

"John 9:1–41: A Narrative Discourse Study." *Occasional Papers on Textlinguistics and Translation* 2 (Fall 1988).

"Inerrancy and Authority of Scripture: Affirmations and Clarifications." *Theological Educator* 37 (1988).

"Houses on Sand, Holy Wars, and Heresies: A Review of the Inerrancy Controversy in the Southern Baptist Convention." *Criswell Theological Review* 2, no. 2 (1988).

"Hab. 2:4 in Rom. 1:17: Some Hermeneutical and Theological Questions." *Wesleyan Theological Journal* 22, no. 2 (1987).

"True Piety in James." *Criswell Theological Review* 1, no. 1 (1986).

"The Christological Hermeneutics of Martin Luther." *Grace Theological Journal* 2, no. 2 (1981).

"Romans 7:14–25: Pauline Tensions in the Christian Life." *Grace Theological Journal* 2, no. 2 (1981).

In addition to many more articles and popular publications, there have been regular columns published in *The Unionite, Renewing Minds*, and *The Trinity Magazine.*

Published tributes for a variety of Christian leaders such as Carl F. H. Henry, Ted Engstrom, Chuck Colson, Fred Shuttlesworth, Pope John Paul II, L. Russ Bush III, Bill Bright, and John R. W. Stott, among others.

B. Chapters in Edited Volumes

"Special Revelation." In *A Theology for the Church*. Edited by Daniel L. Akin. Nashville: B&H, revised 2014.

"A Pauline Theology of the Church." In *The Community of Jesus: A Theology of the Church*. Edited by Christopher Morgan and Ken Easley. Nashville: B&H, 2013.

"Denominationalism: Historical Developments, Contemporary Challenges, and Global Opportunities." In *Why We Belong*. Edited by Anthony Chute, Christopher Morgan, and Robert Peterson. Wheaton: Crossway, 2013.

"The Pauline Epistles." In the *Holman Illustrated Bible Handbook*. Edited by Steve Bond and Jeremy Howard. Nashville: B&H, 2012.

"A. H. Strong," "E. Y. Mullins," "John A. Broadus," "W. T. Conner," and "A. T. Robertson." In *The Encyclopedia of Christian Civilization*. Edited by George T. Kurian. Oxford: Blackwell, 2011.

"The Psalms in Christian Worship." In *Interpreting the Psalms for Teaching and Preaching*. Edited by Herb Bateman and Brent Sandy. St. Louis: Chalice, 2010.

"Convictional, Yet Cooperative." In *The Great Commission Resurgence*. Edited by Chuck Lawless and Adam Greenway. Nashville: B&H, 2010.

"The History of Calvinism in the Southern Baptist Convention." In *Calvinism: A Southern Baptist Dialogue*. Edited by Brad J. Waggoner and E. Ray Clendenen. Nashville: B&H, 2008.

"The Church, Worship, and the Lord's Supper." In *The Mission of Today's Church*. Edited by Stan Norman. Nashville: B&H, 2006.

"Blending Baptist with Orthodox in the Christian University." In *The Future of Baptist Higher Education*. Edited by Donald D. Schmeltekoph and Dianna Vitanza. Waco: Baylor University Press, 2006.

"A. H. Strong." In *Region in Geschichte und Gegenwart*. Tubingen: Mohr, 2004.

"Imputation," "Son of God," "Scripture," and "Revelation of God." In *Holman Illustrated Bible Dictionary*. Edited by C. Brand, C. Draper, and A. England. Nashville: Holman, 2003.

"Worthy Is the Lamb." In *The Battle for Planet Earth: Essays in Honor of Norman Gulley*. Edited by R. duPreez and J. Moskala. Berrien Springs, MI: Andrews University Press, 2003.

"Paul's View of the Spiritual Life." In *Exploring Christian Spirituality: An Ecumenical Reader*. Edited by Kenneth J. Collins. Grand Rapids: Baker, 2000.

"John A. Broadus: Mighty in the Scriptures." In *Biblical Interpreters of the 20th Century: A Selection of Evangelical Voices*. Edited by Walter Elwell. Grand Rapids: Baker, 1999.

"Worship." In *Baptist: Why and Why Not Revisited*. Edited by Timothy George and Richard Land. Nashville: B&H, 1997.

"Dance." In *Dictionary of Old Testament Theology*. Edited by W. VanGemeren. Grand Rapids: Zondervan, 1997.

"Appoint," "Beauty," "Counselor," and "Watchfulness." In *Evangelical Dictionary of Biblical Theology*. Edited by Walter Elwell. Grand Rapids: Baker, 1996.

"Foundations for Reformation Hermeneutics." In *Evangelical Hermeneutics*. Edited by M. Bauman and D. Hall. Camp Hill, PA: Christian Publications, 1995.

"Fruit of the Spirit," and "Old Nature/New Nature." In *Dictionary of Paul and His Letters*. Edited by G. Hawthorne, R. Martin, and D. Reid. Downers Grove: InterVarsity, 1993.

"Preaching and Hermeneutics." In *A Handbook of Contemporary Preaching*. Edited by Michael Duduit. Nashville: Broadman, 1993.

"Hermeneutics for Preaching: A Historical (Author-Oriented) Model." In *Hermeneutics and Preaching*. Edited by Raymond Bailey. Nashville: Broadman, 1993.

"Life in the Spirit in Pauline Thought." In *Scribes and Scriptures: Essays in Honor of J. Harold Greenlee*. Edited by David A. Black. Winona Lake: Eisenbrauns, 1992.

"The Value of Typological Exegesis." In *Restoring the Prophetic Mantle*. Edited by George Klein. Nashville: Broadman, 1992.

"The Environment, Ethics, and Exposition." In *The Earth Is the Lord's*. Edited by Louis Moore and Richard Land. Nashville: Broadman, 1992.

"Baptism." In *Dictionary of Jesus and the Gospels*. Edited by S. McKnight, J. Green, and I. H. Marshall. Downers Grove: InterVarsity, 1991.

"A Theological Foundation for Evangelism." In *Evangelism for the 21st Century: Essays In Honor of Lewis A. Drummond*. Edited by Thom Rainer. Wheaton: Harold Shaw, 1989.

"The Divine-Human Authorship of Inspired Scripture." In *Authority and Interpretation: A Baptist Perspective*. Edited by Duane Garrett and Richard Melick. Grand Rapids: Baker, 1987.

C. Booklets

Building Bridges, with Timothy George. Nashville: Convention, 2007.

Basic Christian Beliefs. Shepherd's Notes Series. Nashville: B&H, 1999.

D. Books Edited

Worldview Study Bible. General editor. Nashville: B&H, forthcoming.

Faith and Learning: A Handbook for Christian Higher Education. Nashville: B&H, 2012. Author of chapter, "Faith and Learning."

Christian Leadership Essentials: A Handbook for Managing Christian Organizations. Nashville: B&H, 2011. Author of introductory and concluding chapters.

Southern Baptist Identity: An Evangelical Denomination Faces the Future. Wheaton: Crossway, 2009. Author of chapter, "Southern Baptists in the 21st Century."

John A. Broadus: A Living Legacy. Co-edited with Roger Duke. Nashville: B&H, 2008. Author of chapter, "John A. Broadus and His Influence on A. T. Robertson and the Southern Baptist Convention."

Shaping a Christian Worldview. Co-edited by Gregory A. Thornbury. Nashville: B&H, 2002. Author of chapter, "Shaping a Christian Worldview."

Theologians of the Baptist Tradition. Co-editor with Timothy George. Nashville: B&H, 2001. Author of chapters, "John A. Broadus and A. T. Robertson," "Herschel Hobbs," and "Looking Back, Looking Ahead."

The Future of Christian Higher Education. Co-editor with David P. Gushee. Nashville: B&H, 1999. Author of four chapters.

Holman Concise Bible Commentary. General editor. Nashville: B&H, 1998.

New Dimensions in Evangelical Thought: Essays in Honor of Millard J. Erickson. Downers Grove: IVP, 1998. Author of chapter, "Millard J. Erickson."

The Best of A. T. Robertson. Compiler. Nashville: B&H, 1996.

The Challenge of Postmodernism: An Evangelical Engagement. Grand Rapids: Baker/ Bridgepoint, 1995, revised 2001. Author of the chapter, "The Challenge of Postmodernism."

Foundations for Biblical Interpretation. Co-editor with Kenneth A. Mathews and Robert B. Sloan. Nashville: B&H, 1994. Author of chapter, "The Study and Interpretation of the Bible."

Southern Baptists and American Evangelicals: The Conversation Continues. Nashville: Broadman, 1993. Author of chapters, "Introduction to Southern Baptists and American Evangelicals" and "Evangelical Responses to Southern Baptists."

Holman Bible Handbook. General editor. Nashville: Holman, 1992. Author of sections, "The Pauline Letters," "History of Biblical Interpretation," "Christian Faith and the Christian Community," and "The Lord's Supper."

Beyond The Impasse? Scripture, Interpretation, and Theology in Baptist Life. Co-editor with Robison B. James. Nashville: Broadman, 1992. Author of the chapter, "A People of the Book: The Crisis of Biblical Authority Today."

New Testament Criticism and Interpretation. Co-editor with David A. Black. Grand Rapids: Zondervan, 1991. Author of chapter, "The History of New Testament Interpretation."

People of God: Essays on the Believers' Church in Honor of James Leo Garrett Jr. Co-editor with Paul A. Basden. Nashville: Broadman, 1991.

Baptist Theologians. Co-editor with Timothy George. Nashville: Broadman, 1990. Author of chapter, "Millard J. Erickson."

E. Books Authored

The Great Tradition of Christian Thinking. With Timothy George. Wheaton: Crossway, 2012.

Southern Baptist Consensus and Renewal: A Biblical, Historical, and Theological Proposal. Nashville: B&H, 2008.

Renewing Minds: Serving Church and Society Through Christian Higher Education. Nashville: B&H, 2007, revised 2008.

Holman Guide to Interpreting the Bible. With George Guthrie. Nashville: B&H, 2004.

Our Christian Hope: Answers to Questions about the Future. Nashville:
    LifeWay, 1998.
Ephesians: One Body in Christ. Nashville: Convention, 1996.
*Christian Scripture: An Evangelical Perspective on Inspiration, Authority, and
    Interpretation.* Nashville: B&H, 1995.
Seeking The Kingdom: The Sermon on the Mount Made Practical. With David E.
    Garland. Wheaton: Harold Shaw, 1992.
Biblical Interpretation Then and Now. Grand Rapids: Baker, 1992.
The Doctrine of the Bible. Nashville: Convention, 1991.

F. Series Edited

New American Commentary. General editor for first six volumes of a projected
    forty-five-volume series. Editor for New Testament volumes. Nashville: B&H,
    1991–present.
Reclaiming the Christian Intellectual Tradition. General editor of projected fif-
    teen-volume series. Wheaton: Crossway, 2012–present.

G. Editorial (Periodicals)

Renewing Minds: A Journal of Christian Thought. Publisher, 2012–present.
Christian Higher Education Journal. Member of editorial board, 2008–13.
Foundations: The Journal of the Religious and Theological Studies Fellowship. Member
    of editorial board, 1997–2000.
Review and Expositor. Editorial Board (1993–95).
Christianity Today. Consulting Editor (1992–2014).
Criswell Theological Review. Co-editor with Kenneth A. Mathews (1985–89).

H. Book Reviews and Endorsements

More than 125 endorsements for books for dozens of different publishers. More
    than 100 book reviews in various periodicals and journals.

III. Select and Representative Listing of Presentations

Day-Higginbotham Lectures at Southwestern Baptist Theological Seminary (2014
    and 1998).
Keynote Address at the Annual Meeting of the Southwest Region of the Evangelical
    Theological Society (2014).
Keynote Address at the Annual Meetings of the University Educators for Global
    Engagement (2014 and 2011).
Duke K. McCall Christian Leadership Lectures at The Southern Baptist
    Theological Seminary (2013).
Commencement Address at Lee University (2013).
Inaugural Academic Address for President Jason Allen at Midwestern Baptist
    Theological Seminary (2013).

Inaugural Address for President Anthony Allen at Hannibal-LaGrange University (2012).

Caskey Distinguished Scholar Lectures at Louisiana College (2012).

Keynote Address at the Annual Meeting of the National Association of Christian Librarians (2012).

Faith and Thought Lectures at Northwestern College (2011).

Faculty Lectures at Beeson Divinity School (2011).

Convocation Address at Dordt College (2011).

Faculty Lectures at Grace College and Seminary (2010).

Plenary Address at the Spiritual Formation Symposium of the Council for Christian Colleges and Universities (2010).

Faculty Lectures at Southwest Baptist University (2010).

20th Anniversary Lectures at Singapore Baptist Seminary/Convention (2010).

Keynote Address at the Annual Meeting of the National Association of Professors of Christian Higher Education (2010).

Strauss Lectures at Lincoln Christian University (2009).

Plenary Address at the Centennial Anniversary of the West Tennessee NAACP.

Hobbs Lectures at Oklahoma Baptist University (2009 and 2001).

Contemporary Issues Lectures at Biola University/Talbot Theological Seminary (2009).

Whiteside Preaching Lectures at Erskine College and Seminary (2009).

Christ and Culture Lectures at California Baptist University (2009).

Convocation Address at Beeson Divinity School (2008).

Commencement Address at Dallas Theological Seminary (2008).

Faculty Lectures at Southeastern Baptist Theological Seminary (2007).

Plenary Address at the Conference on Business, Healthcare, Culture, and Education at Quingdao University in Quingdao, China (2006).

Plenary Address at The Mission of Today's Church Conference at New Orleans Baptist Theological Seminary (2005).

Torrey Lectures at Biola University (2005).

Faculty Lectures at Southern Baptist Theological Seminary (2005).

Hester Lectures at The Association of Southern Baptist Colleges and Schools (2004).

Plenary Address at Worldview Conference, University of Mobile (2004).

Address at the Conference on The Soul of the University at Baylor University (2004).

Inaugural Address for President Evans Whitaker at Anderson University (SC) (2003).

Faculty Lectures at Golden Gate Baptist Theological Seminary (2003).

Keynote Address at Faculty Leadership and Development Conference of the Council for Christian Colleges and Universities (2003).

Trustee Lectures at Azusa Pacific University (2003).

Keynote Address at the Annual Meeting of the Consortium for Global
    Education (2002).
Convocation Address at Houston Baptist University (2002).
Convocation Address at Midwestern Baptist Theological Seminary (2002).
Commencement Address at Azusa Pacific University (2002).
Trustee Lectures at Oklahoma Christian University (2002).
Plenary Address at the Annual Meeting of the Evangelical Theological
    Society (2001).
Powell Lectures at the Baptist College of Florida (2001).
Plenary Address at Wheaton College Theology Conference (2001).
Founders' Day Lecture at Southern Baptist Theological Seminary (2001).
Commencement/Consecration Address at Beeson Divinity School, Samford
    University (1999).
Keynote Address at the 50th Anniversary of the Christian Life Commission of the
    SBC (1996).
Spell Lectures at Mississippi College (1996).
Faculty Lectures at Canadian Southern Baptist Seminary (1994).
Page Lectures at Southeastern Baptist Theological Seminary (1993).
Plenary Address at The Institute for the Study of Protestantism and American
    Culture (1993).
Henderson-Powell Distinguished Christian Scholar Lectures at Mid-America
    Baptist Seminary (1992).
Dimension Lectures at Gardner-Webb University (1991).
Keynote Address at the Annual Meeting of the Southeast Regional Meeting of the
    Evangelical Theological Society (1990).
Numerous chapel addresses and other presentations at other colleges and uni-
    versities. Hundreds of sermons at churches. Dozens of presentations at
    denominational events, including a thematic sermon at the Annual Meeting
    of the Southern Baptist Convention. Speaker at the White House Christian
    Fellowship as well as at the C. S. Lewis Conference at Oxford University.
In addition to this listing of presentations, there have been more than thirty formal
    presidential addresses given at both Union University and Trinity International
    University.

IV. Select Listing of Recognitions

Holman Christian Standard Award. Presented by LifeWay Christian
    Resources (2014).
Distinguished Denominational Service Award. Presented by Midwestern Baptist
    Theological Seminary (2014).
Honorary Doctor of Letters. Presented by Union University (2013).
Honorary Membership, Phi Alpha Theta, for contribution to the discipline of
    history (2013).

Land Distinguished Service Award of the Ethics and Religious Liberty
    Commission (2013).
Hobbs Distinguished Denominational Service Award. Presented by Oklahoma
    Baptist University (2013).
Humanitarian of the Year. Presented by West Tennessee Red Cross (2013).
William D. Smart Race Relations Award. Presented by the West Tennessee
    NAACP (2012).
Man of the Year for Jackson, Tennessee (2008).
Distinguished Alumnus. Southwestern Baptist Theological Seminary (2002).

V. Focus of Research

Subject of doctoral dissertation: "The Integration of Jesus' Great Commandment
    within Christian Higher Education: An Analysis of the Leadership Praxis of
    David S. Dockery," by Tanner Hickman. Southeastern Baptist Theological
    Seminary (2010).
One of ten theologians discussed in "New Voices in Baptist Theology." Pages
    704–12 in *Baptist Theology: A Four-Century Study*, by James Leo Garrett Jr.
    Macon: Mercer University Press, 2009.

VI. Select Listing of Leadership and Service Opportunities

Board of Directors, The King's College (2014–)
Board of Advisors, Gordon College (2013–)
Chair, Southern Baptist Consortium for Intercultural Ministry and
    Education (2013)
Board of Directors, Manhattan Declaration (2012–)
Chair, Southern Baptist Advisory Committee on Calvinism (2012–13)
Board of Directors, Prison Fellowship (2012– ; Board of Reference 2001–11;
    Colson Center 2012–)
Southern Baptist Name Change Task Force (2011–12)
Southern Baptist Great Commission Resurgence Task Force (2009–10)
Board of Directors, Council for Christian Colleges and Universities (2000–2009;
    Chair, 2005–7)
Board of Directors, Christianity Today (2002–6)
Board of Directors, International Association of Baptist Colleges and
    Universities (2006–11)
Board of Directors, Consortium for Global Education (2004–10; Chair, 2006–7)
Board of Directors, Tennessee Independent Colleges and Universities
    Association (2004–7)
Senior Fellow, Research Institute of the Ethics and Religious Liberty
    Commission (1999–)
Southern Baptist InterAgency Coordinating Committee (1993–96)
Southern Baptist Resolutions Committee (1994)

Baptist World Alliance (Heritage and Identity Commission 1993–2003;
    Theological Education Commission 1993–99)
Commissioner, Southern Association of Colleges and Schools (1998–2000)
Publications Committee, Association of Theological Schools (1994–96)
Paul Harris Fellow, Rotary Club

Contributors

Daniel L. Akin, professor of Christian preaching and president, Southeastern Baptist Theological Seminary, Wake Forest, North Carolina

Hunter Baker, associate professor of political science and dean of instruction, Union University, Jackson, Tennessee

Barry H. Corey, president, Biola University, La Mirada, California

Philip W. Eaton, president emeritus, Seattle Pacific University, Seattle, Washington

Millard J. Erickson, theologian at-large and retired dean, Bethel Theological Seminary, Saint Paul, Minnesota

Gene C. Fant Jr., provost and chief academic officer, Palm Beach Atlantic University, West Palm Beach, Florida

Nathan A. Finn, associate professor of historical theology and Baptist studies, Southeastern Baptist Theological Seminary, Wake Forest, North Carolina

James Leo Garrett Jr., distinguished professor of theology emeritus, Southwestern Baptist Theological Seminary, Fort Worth, Texas

Timothy George, founding dean and professor of divinity, Beeson Divinity School, Samford University, Birmingham, Alabama

George H. Guthrie, Benjamin W. Perry professor of Bible, Union University, Jackson, Tennessee

Barbara C. McMillin, president, Blue Mountain College, Blue Mountain, Mississippi

C. Ben Mitchell, provost and vice president for academic affairs, Graves professor of moral philosophy, Union University, Jackson, Tennessee

R. Albert Mohler Jr., Joseph Emerson Brown professor of Christian theology and president, The Southern Baptist Theological Seminary, Louisville, Kentucky

Autumn Alcott Ridenour, assistant professor of religious and theological studies, Merrimack College, North Andover, Massachusetts

Carla D. Sanderson, provost emeritus, Union University and vice president for institutional effectiveness and professional regulation, Chamberlain College of Nursing, Chicago, Illinois

Robert Smith Jr., professor of Christian preaching, Beeson Divinity School, Samford University, Birmingham, Alabama

Carol Swain, professor of political science and law, Vanderbilt University, Nashville, Tennessee

Gregory Alan Thornbury, president, The King's College, New York, New York

Kimberly Thornbury, vice president for institutional research and strategic initiatives, The King's College, New York, New York

Jon R. Wallace, president, Azusa Pacific University, Azusa, California

James Emery White, senior pastor, Mecklenburg Church, Charlotte, North Carolina, and adjunct professor of theology and apologetics, Gordon-Conwell Theological Seminary, Charlotte, North Carolina

John D. Woodbridge, research professor of church history and the history of Christian thought, Trinity Evangelical Divinity School, Deerfield, Illinois

Carl Zylstra, president emeritus, Dordt College, Sioux Center, Iowa

Name Index

Akin, Daniel L.   *133–34, 187*
Aquinas, Thomas   *105*
Augustine   *43, 95–106*
Ayres, Lewis   *98, 103–4*

Baker, Hunter   *viii, 81, 187*
Barth, Karl   *96–101, 104, 106–8, 128*
Basden, Paul A.   *4*
Bell, Peter   *20, 85*
Berry, Wendell   *x–xi*
Bettenson, Henry   *96–97*
Black, David Alan   *4, 7, 95*
Blagojevich, Rod   *120*
Bloom, Allan   *21*
Bodie, Graham D.   *28*
Bonomi, Patricia U.   *84–85*
Brooks, Arthur C.   *23*
Brownstein, Ronald   *20*
Bullock, John G.   *26*

Cahill, Lisa Sowle   *101*
Carlson, David Gray   *27*
Carter, Stephen L.   *72*
Castiglione, Baldesar   *70*
Cathcart, William   *111*
Cavanaugh, Thomas A.   *115*

Collins, Jimmy   *68, 70, 75*
Constant, Benjamin   *85–86*
Cooley, Michael   *68*
Corey, Barry H.   *137, 187*
Cornelius, R. H.   *66*
Cromwell, Oliver   *31*
Cubberley, Ellwood Patterson   *123*
Curlin, Farr A.   *115–16*

Daly, Brian   *97–98*
Derrida   *27*
Dillenberger, John   *105*
Dockery, David   *viii–xi, 3–9, 11, 14–16, 18–19, 67, 74, 77–79, 83, 93, 96, 109, 124–31, 137, 140, 142–44, 147–48, 150–51, 153–57, 161–73*
Donno, Daniel   *71*
Dreisbach, Daniel L.   *110, 114*
Drucker, Peter F.   *89–90*
Dworkin, Ronald   *40*

Early, Joseph E.   *110, 114*
Eaton, Philip W.   *141, 187*
Eberstadt, Mary   *42–43*
Eliot, T. S.   *126*
Emmons, Robert A.   *107*

Engelhardt, H. Tristram   *117*
Erickson, Millard J.   *viii, 4, 17, 19,*
   146, 187

Fant, Gene C.   *viii, 67, 187*
Finn, Nathan A.   *145, 187*
Fish, Stanley   *21*
Fitzgerald, Allan D.   *98*

Garrett, James Leo, Jr.   *viii, 4, 14,*
   16, 125, 129, 169, 187
Gaustad, Edwin S.   *111*
George, Timothy   *viii, 4–5, 11, 17,*
   98, 113–14, 125, 146, 187
Gerber, Alan S.   *26*
Gland, Scott   *20*
Gossip, Arthur John   *53*
Green, R.P.H.   *96*
Gregory, Eric   *26, 78, 100, 188*
Guinness, Os   *85–88, 127*
Gushee, David P.   *4*
Guthrie, George H.   *149, 187*

Hall, Mark David   *110, 114*
Helwys, Thomas   *110*
Henry, Carl F. H.   *16–17, 37–38,*
   96, 100, 124
Hick, John   *24*
Hill, Edmund   *100*
Hill, Seth J.   *26*
Hinson, E. Glenn   *16*
Hollenbach, David   *96*
Hollinger, David A.   *39–40*
Holmes, Obadiah   *111–12*
Huber, Gregory A.   *26*
Hunsinger, George   *98*
Hunter, James Davison   *40*
Hutchinson, Paul   *23*
Huxley, Aldous   *88*

James, Robison B.   *4*
Javitch, Daniel   *70*
Johnson, Philip F.   *87*

Kant, Immanuel   *123*
Kessler, Andy   *91–92*
Kronman, Anthony   *90, 92*

Lantos, John   *115*
Lawrence, Ryan E.   *115*
Leland, John   *112–14*
Lewis, C. S.   *81, 98, 102–3*
Lopez, Shane J.   *107*
Luther, Martin   *56, 61, 105*

Machiavelli   *71*
Marty, Martin E.   *139*
Mathewes, Peter W.   *97*
Mathews, Kenneth A.   *4*
Maxwell, John C.   *67*
McKenny, Gerald   *100*
McMillin, Barbara C.   *153, 187*
McNeill, John T.   *105*
Miller, James Andrew   *123*
Mitchell, C. Ben   *viii, 109, 128,*
   187
Mohler, R. Albert   *14, 35, 72, 124,*
   188
Morris, Ryan   *20*
Mouw, Richard J.   *139*

Neder, Adam   *104*
Norris, Richard A.   *97*
Novak, David   *73*

O'Donovan, Oliver   *96*

Pelikan, Jaroslav   *52*
Pitts, Margaret J.   *28*

Ridenour, Autumn Alcott   *viii, 95,*
    101, 188
Rorty, Richard   *24*
Rosell, Garth   *138*
Rosenfeld, Michel   *27*
Rusch, William G.   *97*

Sanderson, Carla D.   *xi, 128, 188*
Shelton, Charles M.   *107*
Shurden, Walter B.   *110*
Simon, Stephanie   *21, 115*
Singleton, Charles S.   *70*
Sloan, Robert B.   *4*
Smith, James K. A.   *126–27*
Smith, Jr., Robert   *viii, 47, 52, 188*
Smith, Michael E., Sr.   *110*
Snyder, C. R.   *107*
Socha, Thomas J.   *28*
Sommerville, C. John   *90*
Sulmasy, Daniel P.   *119*
Swain, Carol   *157, 188*

Tanner, Kathryn   *102, 105*
Taylor, Charles   *40–42*

Thiel, Peter   *91–92*
Thornbury, Gregory Alan   *4*
Thornbury, Kimberly   *78, 80, 123,*
    161, 188
Trueblood, D. Elton   *93*
Truett, George W.   *68, 113–14*
Tull, James E.   *16*

Valentine, Foy   *16*
Vischer, Robert K.   *118–21*

Wallace, Jon R.   *165, 188*
Webster, John   *98*
Wetzel, James   *99–100*
White, James Emery   *169, 188*
Williams, Rowan   *97, 103,*
    109–11
Woodard, Kenneth L.   *16*
Woodbridge, John D.   *171, 188*

Yoe, Mary Ruth   *32*

Zylstra, Carl   *173, 188*
Zyman Sergio   *74–75*

Subject Index

A

abortion *115*
American exceptional-
  ism *87*
Amyraldian *9–10*
annihilationism *10*
Arminianism *9–10*

C

Calminian *9–10*
Calvinism *9, 147*
civil *25, 95, 139,*
  149, 153–55
civility *14, 19,*
  22–23, 33–34,
  128–29,
  137–40, 153
common good *vii,*
  90, 108, 119,
  121, 127, 154
conciliation *15*
convictional civility *vii,*
  19, 24, 26,
  95–96, 109,
  129, 170

conviction, conviction-
  al *15, 24–25,*
  35–36, 45–46,
  67–73, 77, 79,
  109, 115, 121,
  128–29, 137,
  139, 154–55,
  174

E

eschatology *9*

H

heaven *10*
hell *10*

I

inerrancy *8, 14*

L

liberty *84–85, 93,*
  112, 118, 121,
  146

R

religious liberty *109–*
  10, 114

S

Second London Con-
  fession *9*

T

tolerance *24–25*

U

universalism *10*

Scripture Index

Genesis

1:26 *47*
2:7 *47*
2:19 *48*
37:17 *49–50*

Exodus

20:3 *102*

Ruth

4:17 *50*

2 Samuel

12:1–14 *30*

Psalms

8:5 *47*
23:2 *64*
23:4 *64, 76*
51:8 *64*
77:19 *51*
100:3 *64*

Proverbs

25:11 *15*

Ecclesiastes

12:7 *47*

Isaiah

9:6 *51*
55:8–9 *31, 52*

Jeremiah

12:5 *53*

Ezekiel

3:17–19 *63*
33:1–6 *63*

Hosea

11:1 *50*

Matthew

2:15 *50*
4:4 *56*
5:44 *34*
7:15 *48*
10:24 *123*
10:26 *46*
10:27 *45–46*
10:33 *31*
16:24 *30–31*
19:19 *34*
22:37 *48*
25:21 *72*
26:34–35, 75 *31*
28:18–20 *35*

Mark

3:13 *48*
8:34 *30–31*
12:30 *102*
14:30–31, 72 *31*
15:34 *51*
16:15–16 *47*

Luke

9:23 *30–31*
10:25–37 *30*
19:41 *59*
22:34, 61 *31*
24:13–36 *53*
24:25 *53*
24:26 *61*
24:32 *53*
24:33–35 *53*

193

John

1:14 *51*
1:17 *63*
3:8 *51*
3:16 *43*
6:60, 66 *62*
6:67–68 *62*
10:27 *106*
11:24 *55*
11:25–26 *55*
11:35 *59*
14:5 *55*
14:6 *55, 61*
14:16 *76*
16:32–33 *106*
17:11, 16 *95*
18:38 *55*
19:30 *62*

Acts

2:22–24 *50*
2:24 *51*
2:41 *52, 54*
4:12 *61*
4:20 *57*
13:14 *58*
13:36 *69*
17:16 *58*
19:1–2 *58*
19:3–4 *58*
19:4–6 *58*
19:9–10 *49, 60*
19:23–31 *58*
20:7–12 *60*
20:17 *58*
20:17–38 *47, 57–58*
20:18 *64*
20:20 *49, 59–60*
20:21 *61*
20:22 *61*

20:23 *61*
20:24 *62–63*
20:25 *48, 63*
20:26 *63*
20:27 *49, 63*
20:28 *64*
20:28–30 *63*
20:29 *64*
20:30 *48, 64*
20:31 *48, 59, 65*
20:33 *65*
20:34 *65*
20:35 *65*
20:36 *65*
20:36–38 *48*
20:37 *59, 63, 65*
20:38 *65*
26:26 *63*

Romans

1:16 *61*
5:1 *56*
5:12–21 *98*
8:11 *51*
11:33–34 *51, 57*

1 Corinthians

10:31 *56*
13:12 *31*
16:19 *60*

2 Corinthians

4:4 *31*
4:6 *31*
11:24–29 *59*

Galatians

3:24 *63*

Ephesians

2:8 *56*
4:14 *48, 154*

Philippians

1:21 *11*
2:8 *59*

Colossians

1:15–16 *97*
1:15–20 *97*
1:17 *98, 159*
2:3 *103*
2:6–7 *95–97, 103, 105*
2:7 *106*
2:8 *107*
3:9–10 *107*
3:12–13 *108*
3:12, 14 *143*

1 Thessalonians

1:3 *61*

1 Timothy

2:5 *56, 61*

2 Timothy

2:17–18 *64*
3:16 *56*
3:16–17 *6, 59*
4:7 *62*

Titus

2:13 *129*

Hebrews

12:2 *62*

1 Peter

1:18–19   *64*
2:9   *43*
3:15   *139*
5:3   *64*

2 Peter

3:9   *54*

Revelation

3:20   *15*

11:15   *46*
13:8   *51*
22:4   *65*